SPREAD
KINDNESS

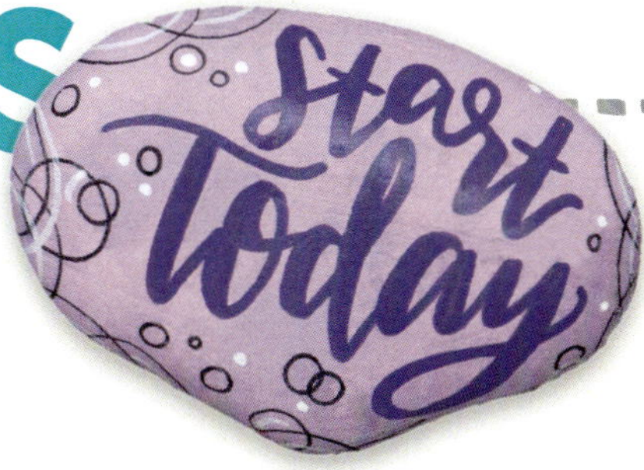

SHARE Joy

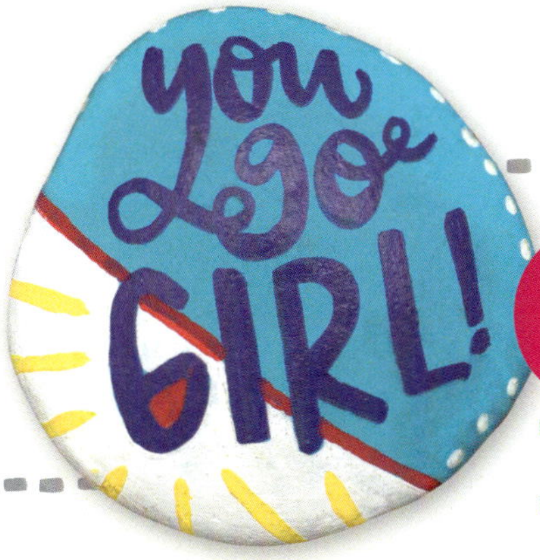

GIVE
Encouragement

I0893791

LEISURE ARTS, INC. • Maumelle, Arkansas

Rock painting

has quickly become one of the hottest new trends in the world of arts and crafts, not only because adorning a rock is a relatively quick and easy project, but also because simple garden pebbles painted with sayings, phrases,and images are unique, cute, and motivational! And for a little extra glitz, simply add Diamond Dotz® Gems.

In this book you will find 30 inspirational rock projects, painted in themed color schemes and decorated with hand lettered sentiments, that will really get you

ROCKIN'!

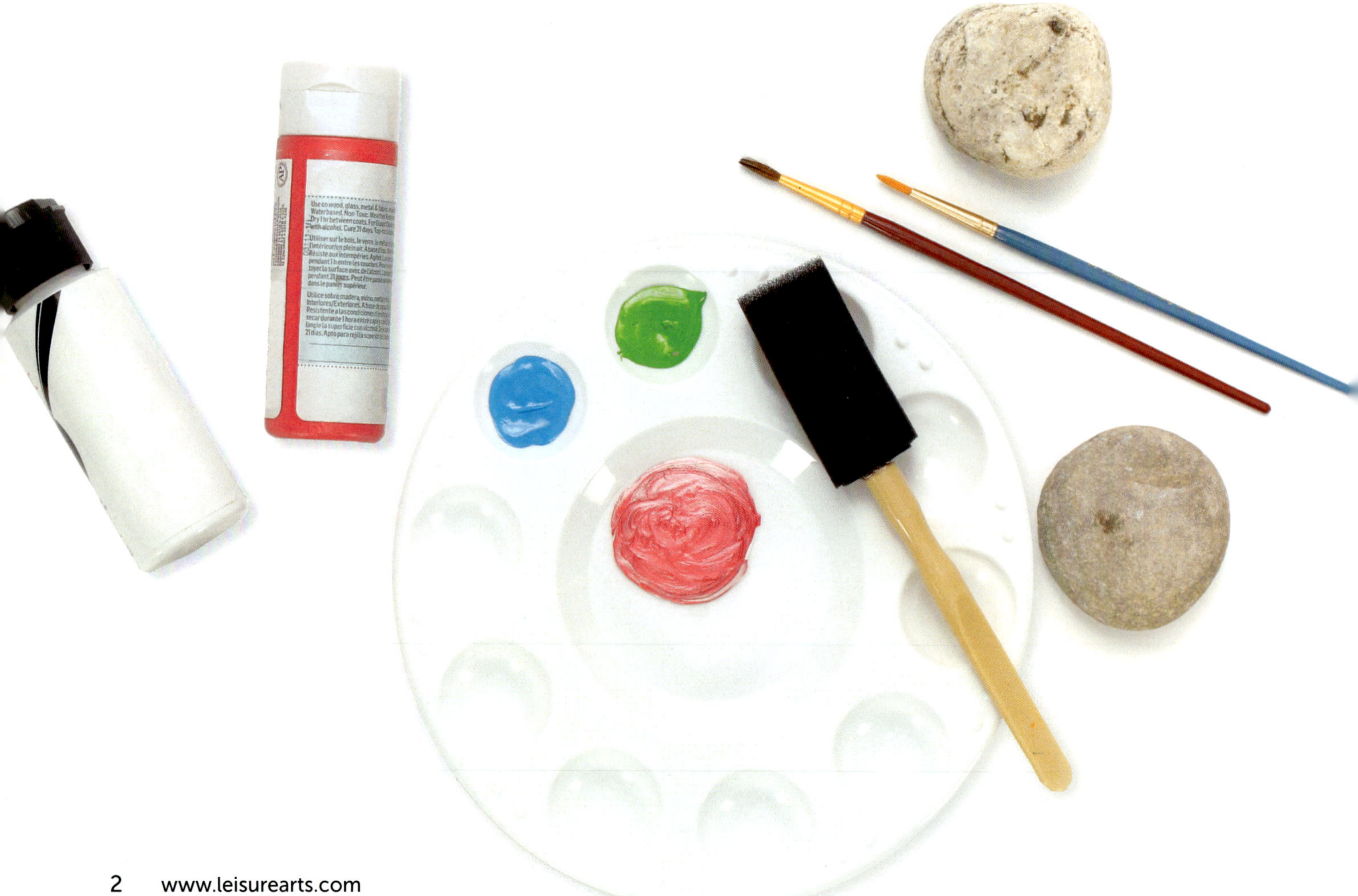

Table of Contents

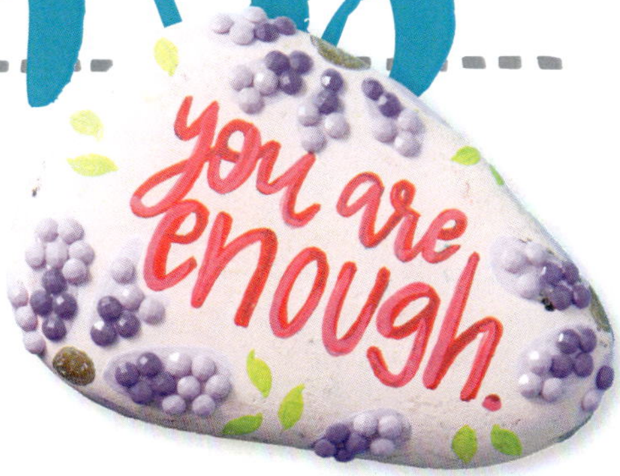

Rock Basics

Selecting rocks for your painted rock projects is one of the most important steps in the process! The rocks used in this book came from a bag of assorted Caribbean beach pebbles (available at almost any home improvement store) but if you can't find any there, craft stores also carry small garden stones for the precise purpose of painting. Even try looking in your garden or backyard.

When choosing rocks for your projects, you want to select rocks that have a smooth surface, with limited cracks, craters, or inconsistent bumps. You want all of your rocks to be different shapes and sizes so that you have a nice variety, but a relatively flat surface is best for painting (especially when it comes to adding small, delicate hand lettering).

All of the rocks featured in this book are smaller than the palm of an average adult hand but please feel free to use any size rocks that your heart desires—if you want to take your projects to a grander scale, go for it!

To prepare your rocks for painting, all you will really need or want to do beforehand is to wash them thoroughly (especially if you are buying your rocks from a home improvement store where they are probably being kept outside). You want a nice, clean surface to apply your paint...one without any excess dust or dirt.

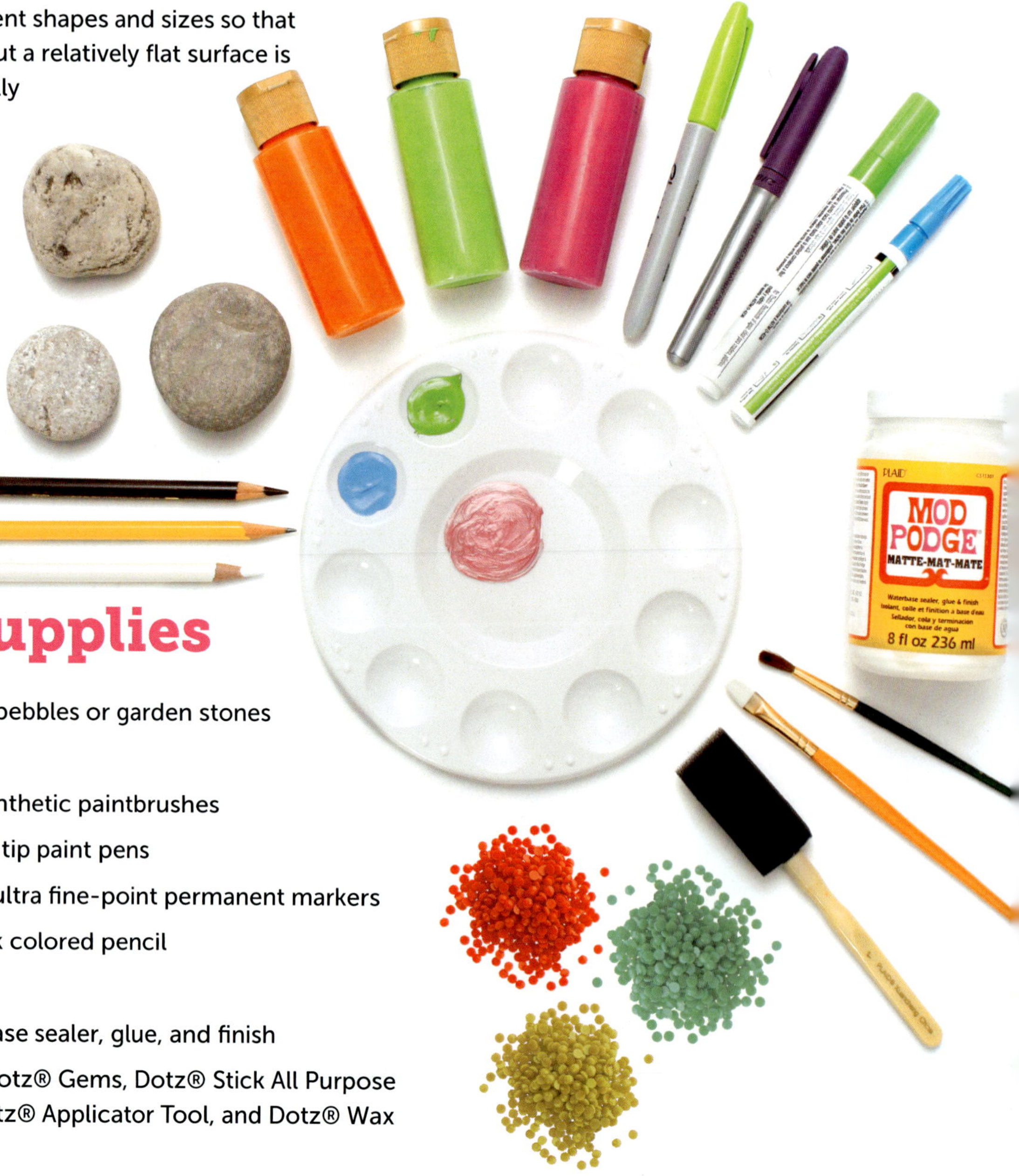

Tools & Supplies

- ☐ small rocks – beach pebbles or garden stones
- ☐ acrylic paint
- ☐ small and medium synthetic paintbrushes
- ☐ fine tip and extra fine tip paint pens
- ☐ black fine-point and ultra fine-point permanent markers
- ☐ #2 lead pencil or dark colored pencil
- ☐ white colored pencil
- ☐ Mod Podge® waterbase sealer, glue, and finish
- ☐ Optional: Diamond Dotz® Gems, Dotz® Stick All Purpose Dotting Adhesive, Dotz® Applicator Tool, and Dotz® Wax

Painting

The best rock projects start with a very solid basecoat of paint. Depending on what brand and color of the paint you are using, you may need to apply multiple coats of paints to any area of your rock for a consistent, solid finish.

Acrylic paints are best for rock painting because they allow more range of color and ease of use than other types of paint (acrylics tend to be much cheaper, as well). The paints used on the projects in this book were not expensive or "name brand," so you do not need to feel obligated to spend a fortune on these projects.

Lettering

When lettering your rocks, feel free to use both paint pens with varying tip sizes or small paintbrushes and paint. The lettering in the projects you will see in this book used both methods of application.

If you are a beginner in the world of hand lettering, it always helps to not only practice on paper beforehand but also to lightly sketch out your lettering on your rock with a pencil before you go in with paint. Not only does that help you mimic your lettering for the final product, it will also help you get your composition the way you want it.

When lettering in one of the calligraphy/cursive styles, a steady, fluid motion is key to connecting your letters. Study and follow the arrows in the "Calligraphy" font, pages 6 & 8, for example, to get used to the motions of the modern cursive fonts.

To make your script look like professional calligraphy (even if you've never done any lettering before), try this "fauxlligraphy" method: write your word, phrase, or quote in pencil, trace with a paint pen or with paint and a paintbrush, then go back and make just the right side of each letter a little thicker than it was before. This method will give you a beautiful calligraphy effect.

Doodling

Doodles add special, unique flair to your projects, and can be anything you want them to be! From dainty flowers and flourishes to geometric shapes and patterns, doodles not only fill space on your rocks, but also make them super interesting to look at. On page 16 you will find little doodles you can copy, practice, or use as inspiration for not only the projects in this book, but any you may create in the future.

Dotting

Gems add just the right amount of sparkle and shine to your painted rocks. Carefully brush the adhesive on the areas you want to apply gems to; you should see a milky white layer of adhesive on the surface. Allow the adhesive to dry until it is clear. Apply the gems to the adhesive as desired.

Sealing

Sealing your rocks is a very important step, especially if you are planning to leave your projects outside in the elements. Applying a few coats of Mod Podge® to your finished projects is a quick and perfect way to seal your rocks so that no damage comes to the hard work you have put in; it comes in both matte and gloss finishes to give you just the look you want.

It is suggested that you apply at least two coats of sealer to the entire rock so that your paint never fades, scuffs, or flakes. Also, don't forget to put your signature on your finished project before applying the sealer so that your work is forever tied to you!

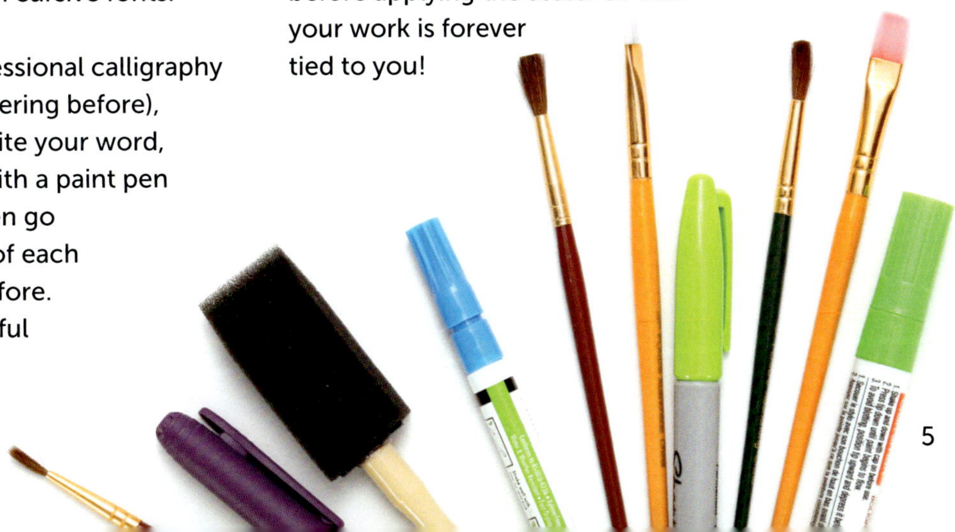

The Calligraphy Font

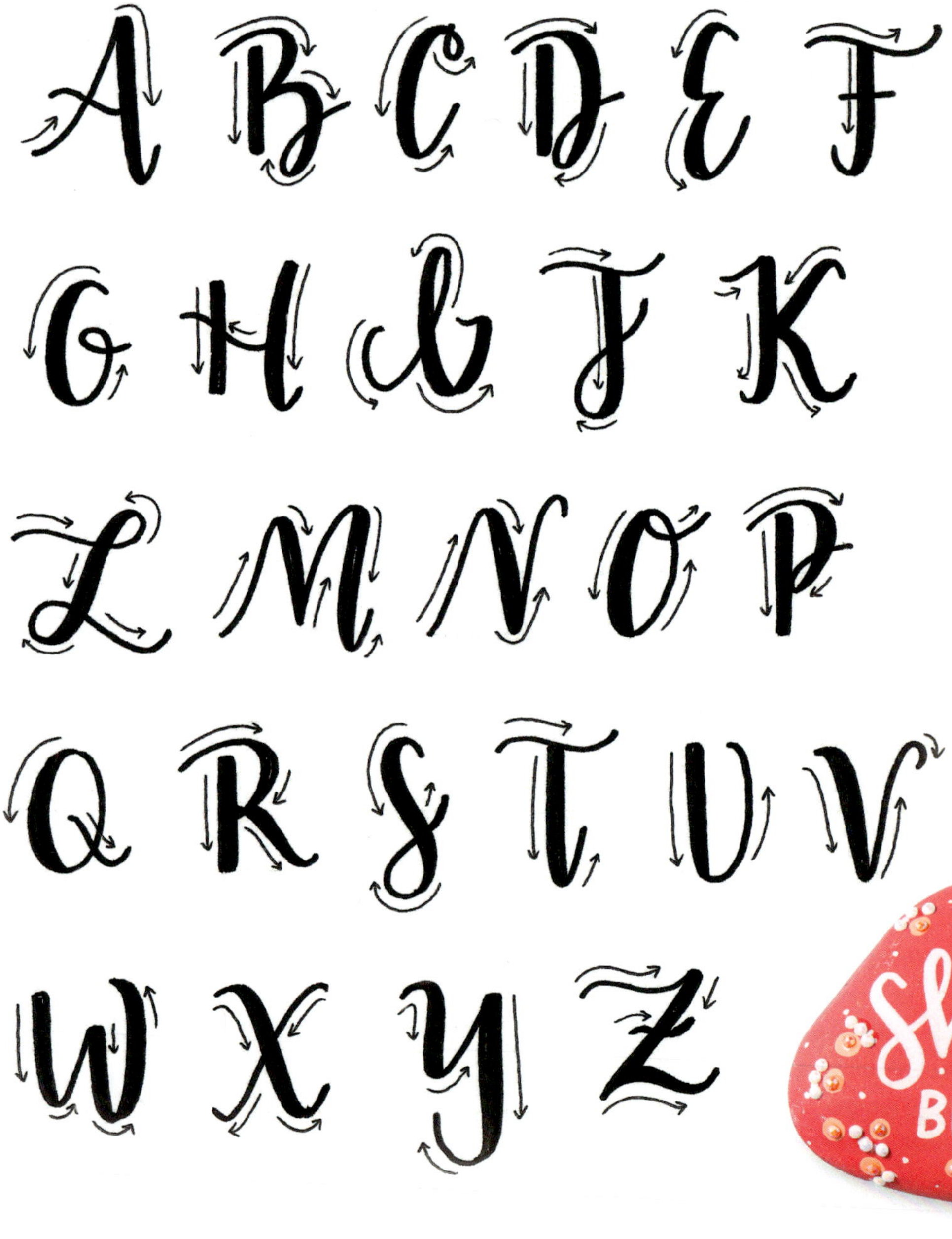

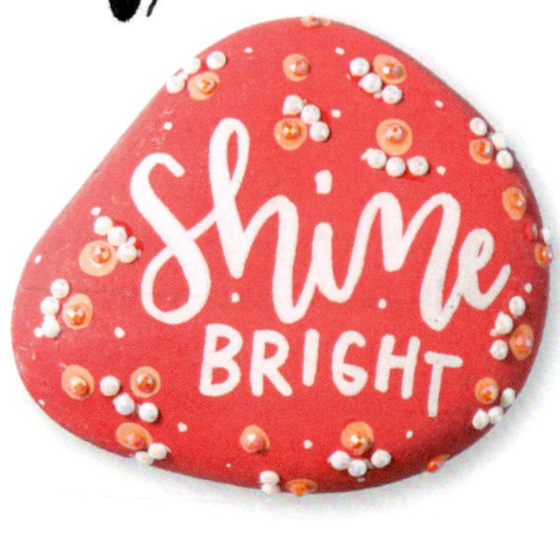

Practice your Lettering Here

The Calligraphy Font

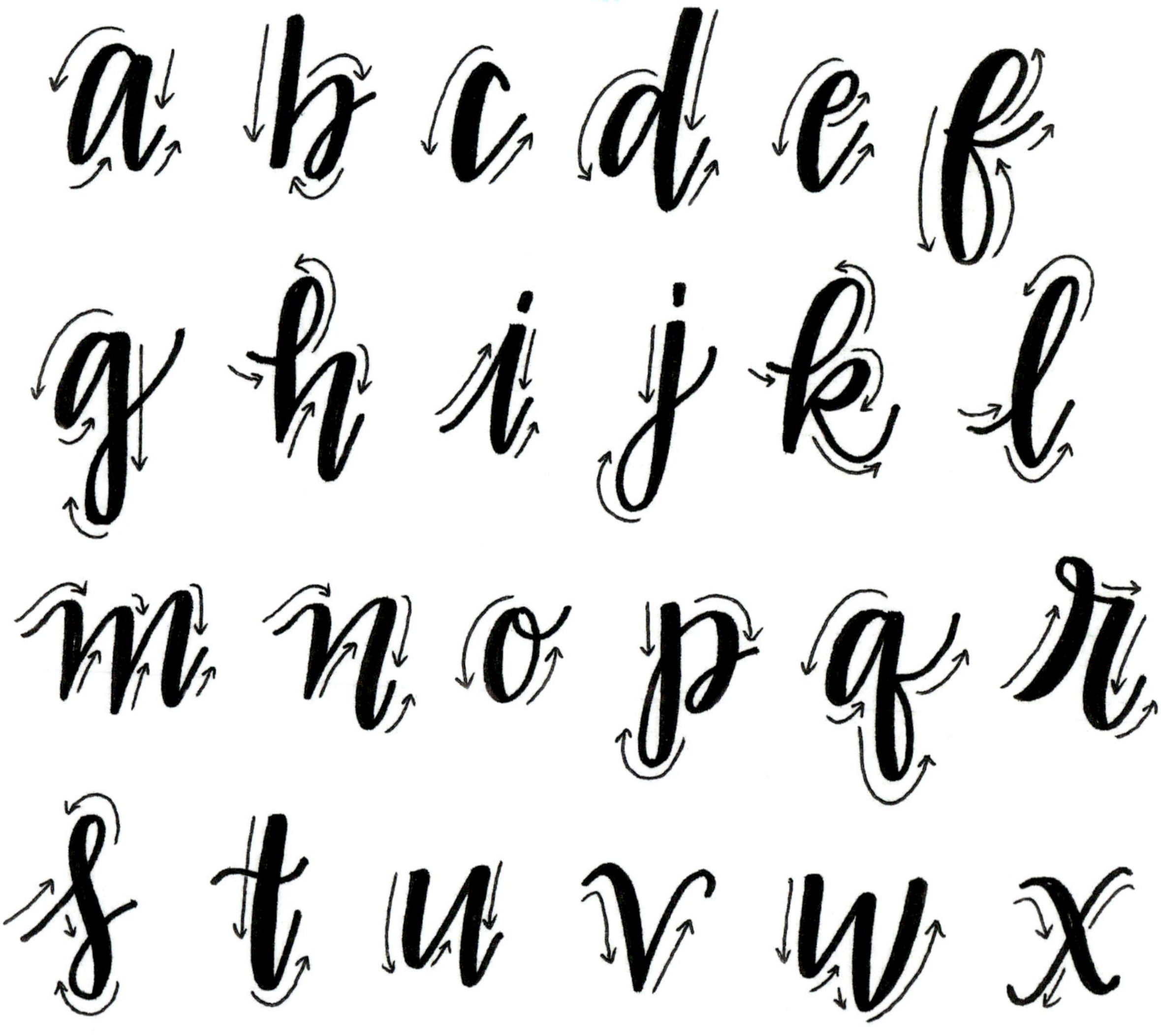

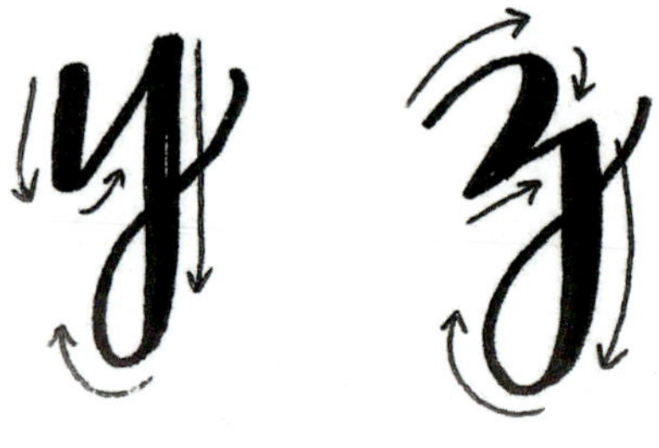

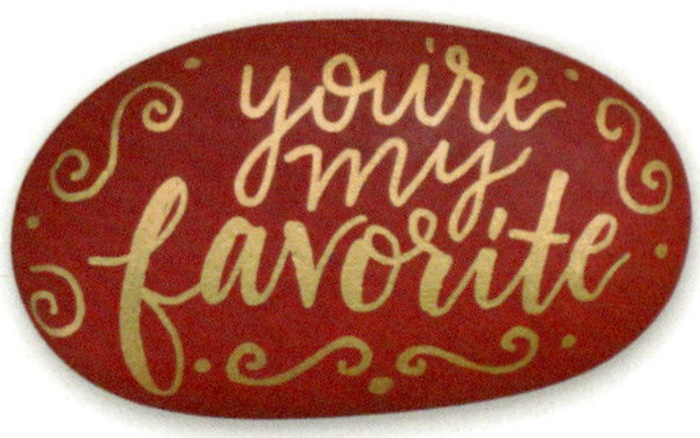

Practice your Lettering Here

The Flirty Font

a b c d e f

g h i j k

l m n o

p q r s t

u v w x y

z

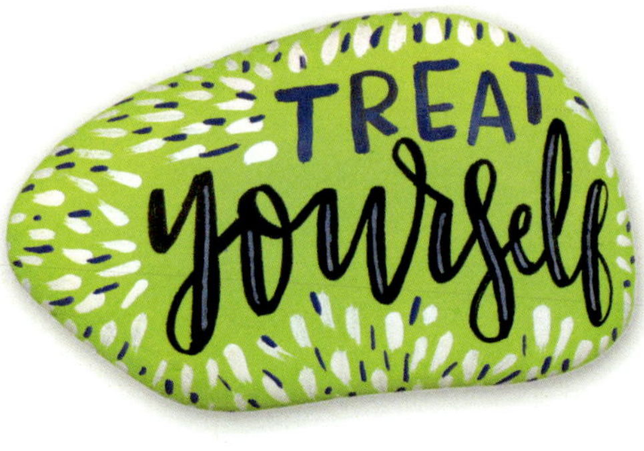

Practice your Lettering Here

The Modern Font

Aa Bb Cc Dd

Ee Ff Gg Hh

Ii Jj Kk Ll

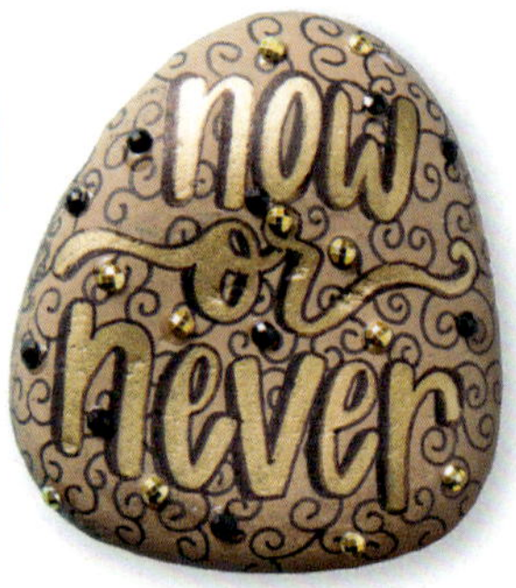

Mm Nn Oo Pp

Qq Rr Ss Tt Uu

Vv Ww Xx Yy Zz

Practice your Lettering Here

The Modern Font

Aa Bb Cc Dd

Ee Ff Gg Hh

Ii Jj Kk Ll

Mm Nn Oo

Pp Qq Rr

Ss Tt Uu Vv

Ww Xx Yy Zz

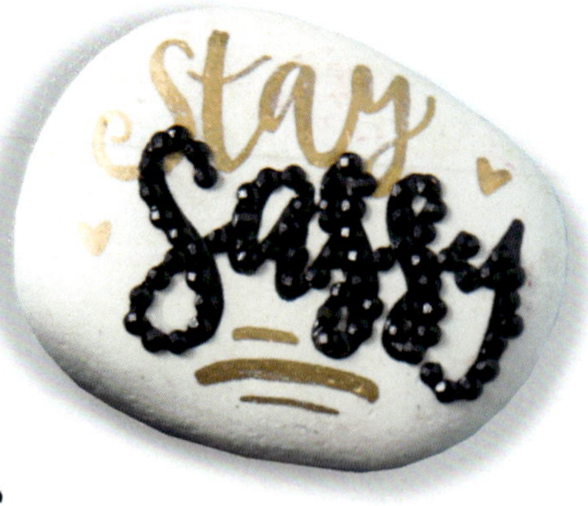

Practice your Lettering Here

Doodle Art

Practice your Doodles Here

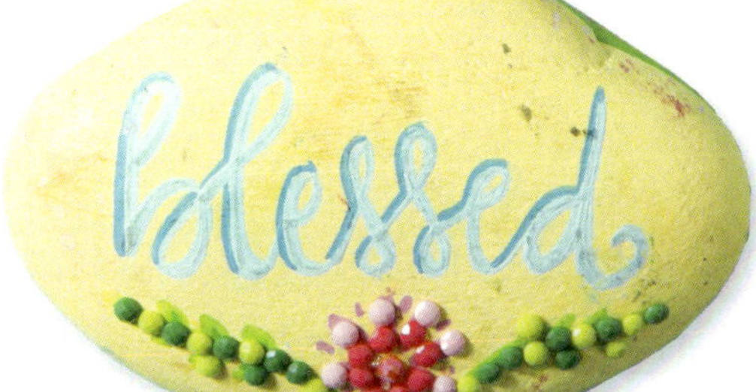

Inspiration ROCKS

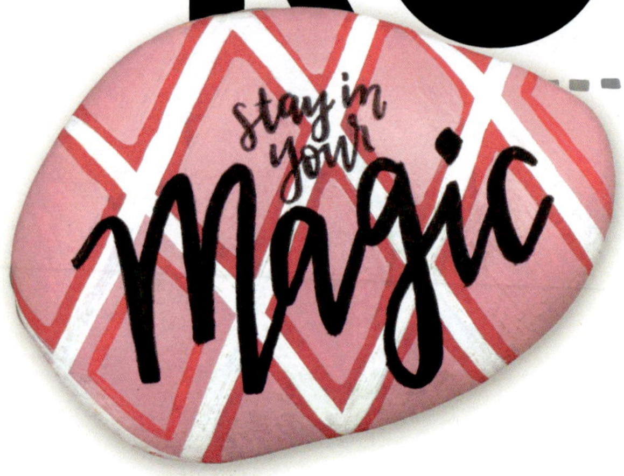

If you can dream it . . .

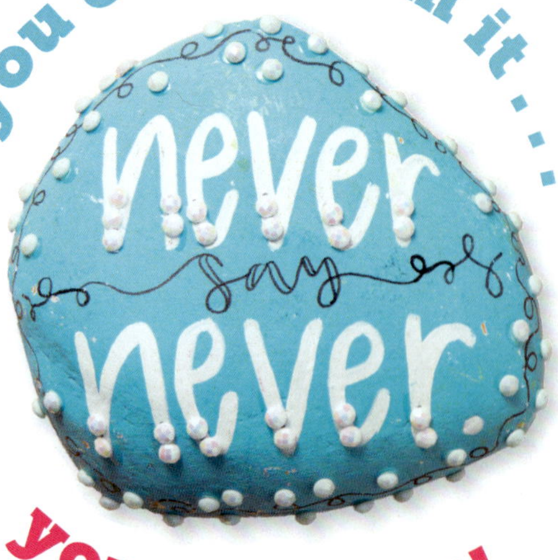

you can do it!

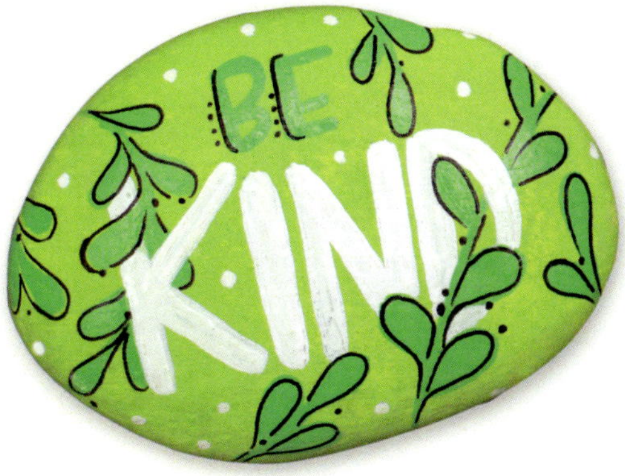

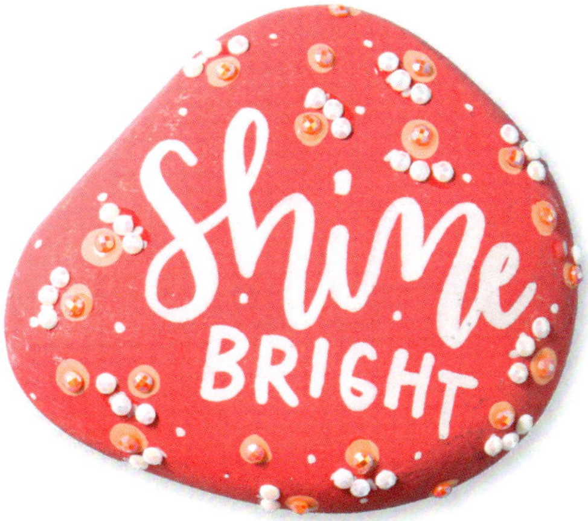

Painted rocks have become
such fun little projects
for so many people because they can act as
tokens of inspiration.

From a rock that says "never say never" to one that motivates you to do something kind for others, spreading or receiving a positive message can really turn a person's day around. In this section you will find six designs that will inspire you to look on the bright side.

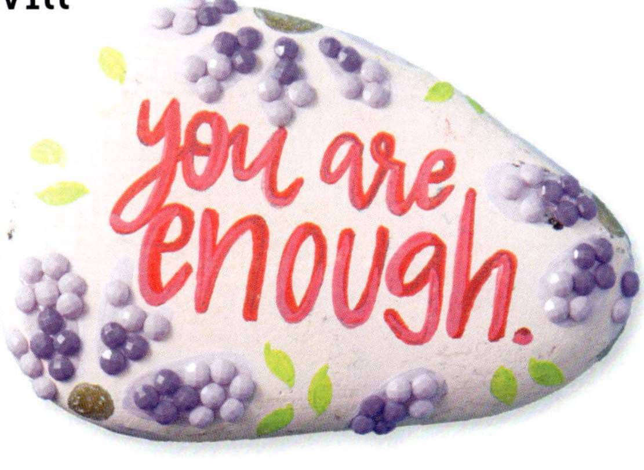

Let's Create the Embrace It Rock

What you need

- ☐ wide, rectangular rock
- ☐ acrylic paint (I used turquoise blue and lime green.)
- ☐ small and medium synthetic paintbrushes
- ☐ green fine tip paint pen
- ☐ black ultra fine-point and fine-point permanent markers
- ☐ #2 lead pencil or dark colored pencil
- ☐ fine tip and extra-fine tip paint pens (I used green.)

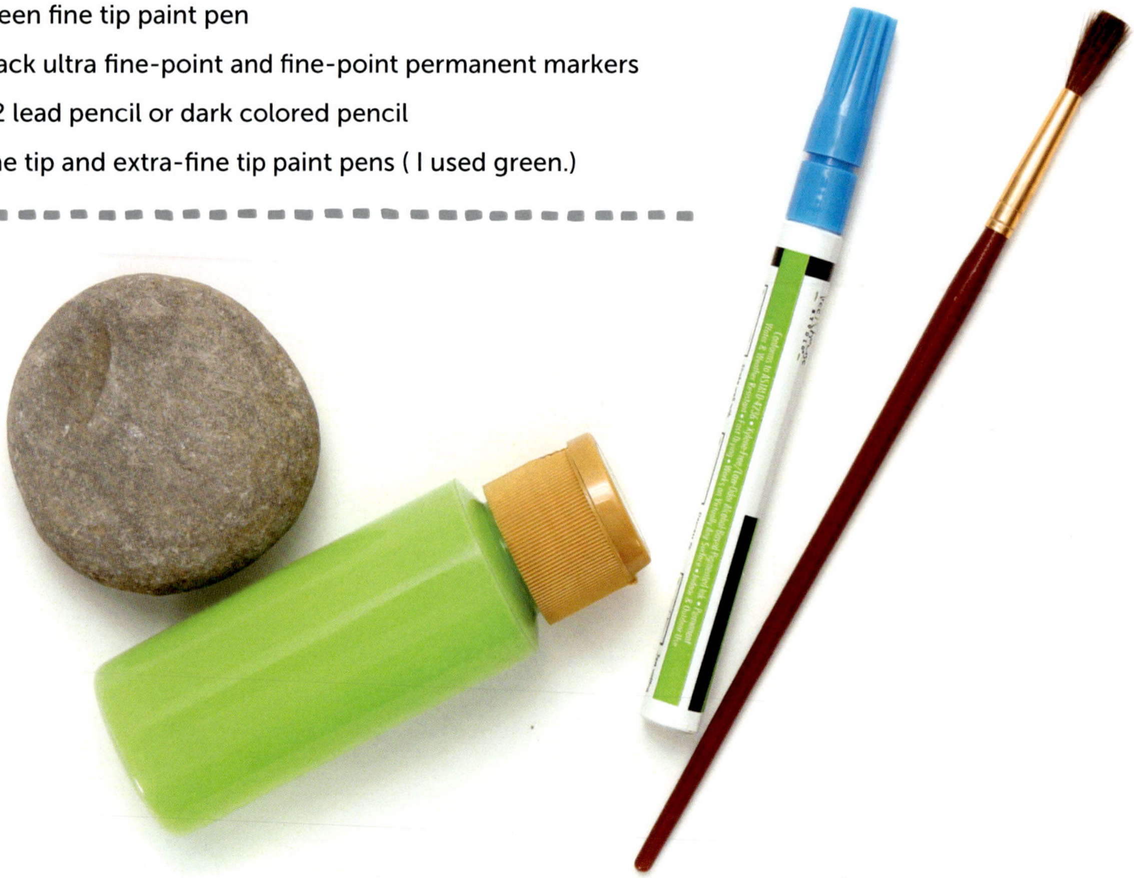

What to do:

1

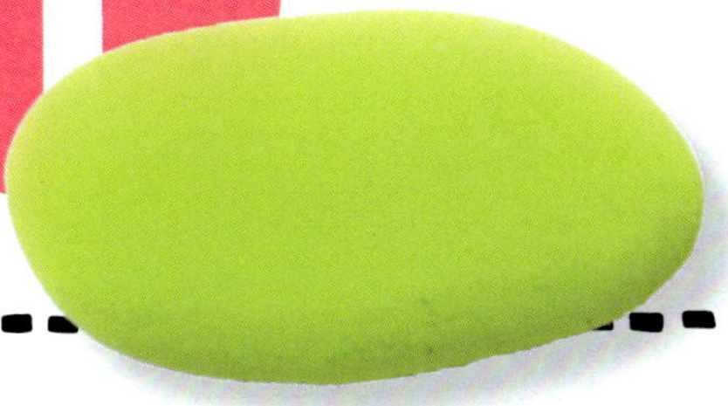

Use the medium paintbrush to paint a double-layer of lime green paint for basecoat.

2

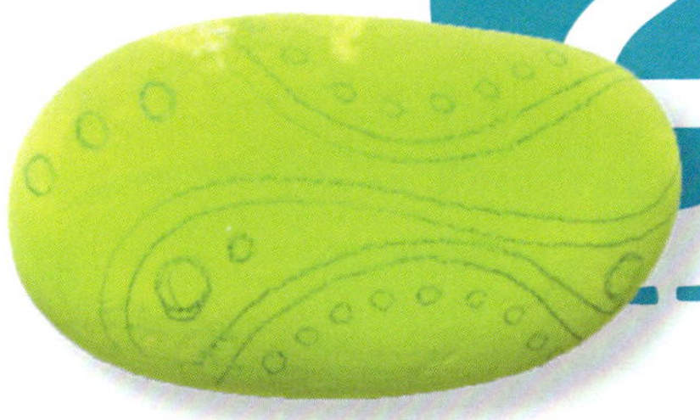

Starting from the left, use a #2 pencil or dark colored pencil to draw a slightly curved wave shape across the center of the rock. Create two more curved lines above and below your center wave line. Sketch some dots in the areas between and alongside the curved lines.

3

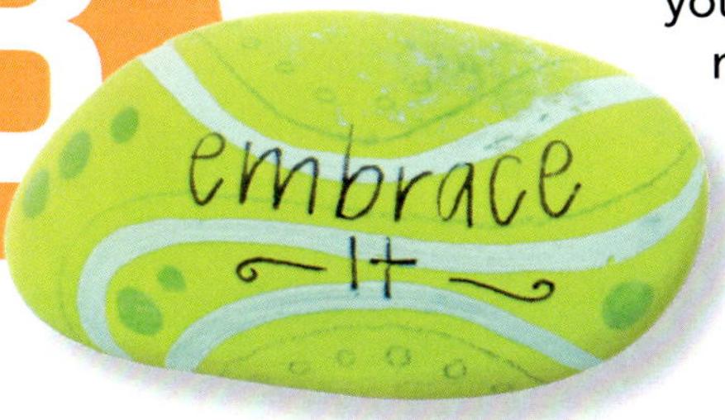

Use the small paintbrush to paint over your drawn lines with turquoise blue paint. Once you are satified, use the ultra fine-point marker to sketch your lettering using the MODERN ALPHABET.

4

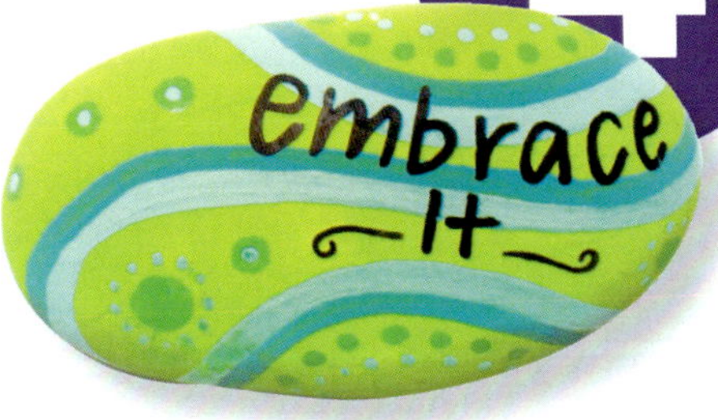

Use the green paint pen to add curved wave lines across the rock. Use the green paint pen and the turquoise blue paint to add circle embellishments and then the fine-point marker to finalize the lettering.

Be *inspired!*

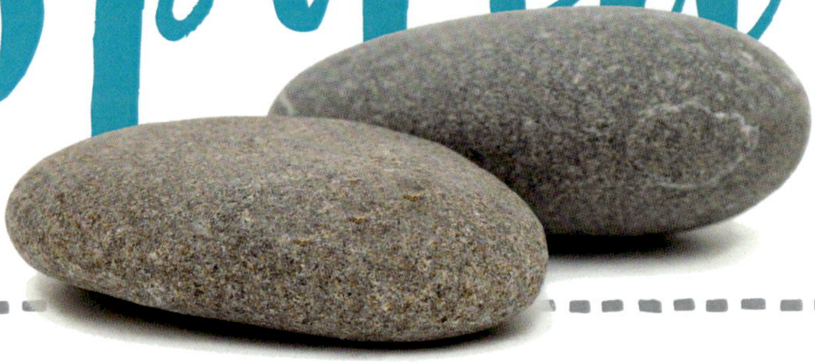

Stay In Your Magic

If you're struggling to get through the week, take a look at this rock on your vanity and remember to stay in your magic;

YOU BRING SOMETHING SPECIAL TO THE TABLE THAT NO ONE ELSE HAS.

Using a medium paintbrush, paint your entire rock in dark pink. Next, add a thick crisscross pattern with a white fine tip paint pen. When dry, use a small paintbrush and pink paint to create diamond shapes in the negative spaces of the crisscross pattern. Use a black fine-point permanent marker and a black fine tip paint pen to add your lettering.

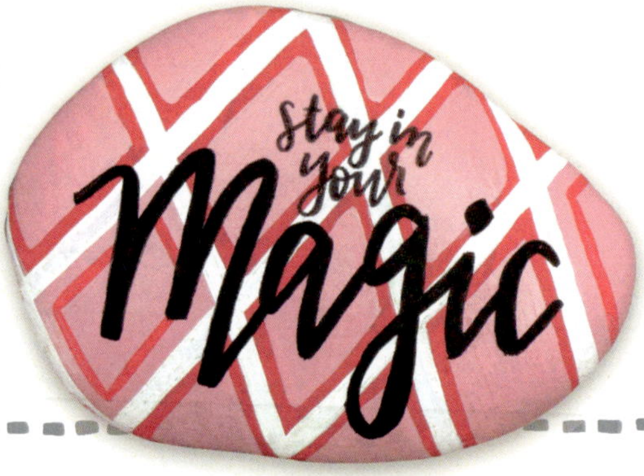

Be Kind

Sometimes the day feels a million years long and it's hard to put on a brave face when someone is getting on our last nerve. But hey, we're all in this together and we all have different obstacles to face.

BE A FRIEND AND BE KIND.

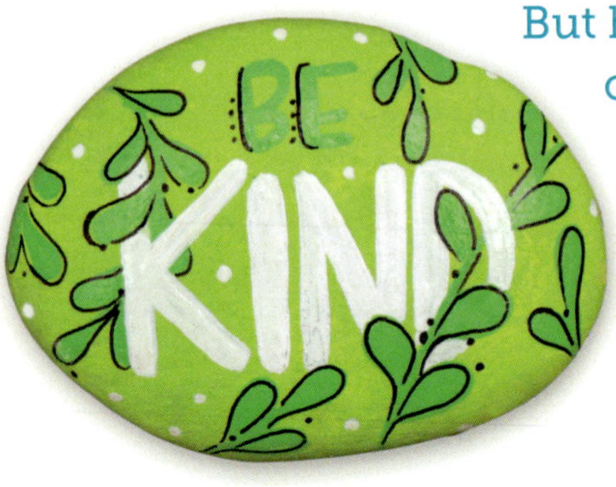

Use a medium paintbrush to paint a double-layer of bright green for your background and use green and white fine tip paint pens to lay down your lettered phrase. Doodle in some leafy vines with paint pen and outline/embellish with a black fine-point permanent marker.

You Are Enough

You are enough, plain and simple. You are worthy of love, of kindness, of respect, of admiration.

LIKE A FLOWER, YOU ARE UNIQUE AND WONDERFULLY MADE.

Celebrate who you are and what makes you, **YOU.**

Paint a solid pink background and use a dark pink fine tip paint pen to establish your lettering. Paint some soft lavender flowers and green leaves around the outside and, when you are happy with your design, add some purple shading for the final touch. Embellish the petals using purple and lavender gems.

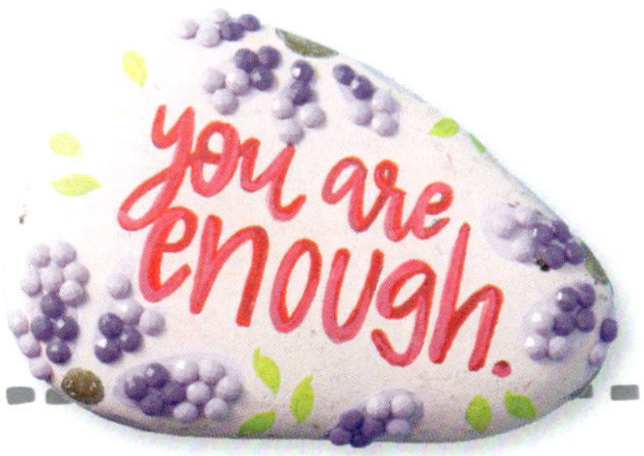

Shine Bright

Every day you are given the opportunity to be a shining source of light in your life and the lives of others...

SO YOU BETTER SHINE BRIGHT!

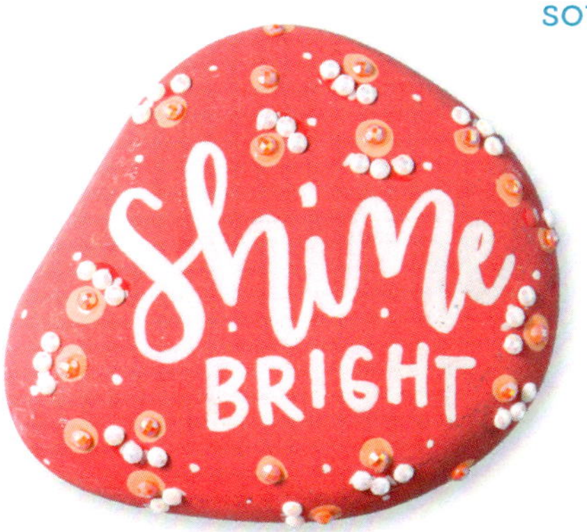

Use a medium paintbrush and vibrant pink paint to paint your solid background. Use a white fine tip paint pen to incorporate bold lettering to make this piece really pop. Add little star-shine elements around your message using a small paintbrush and orange and white paint and a black ultra fine-point marker for a whimsical feel. To make your starry elements shine even brighter, add orange and white gems.

Never Say Never

A tale as old as time: you can do whatever it is you put your mind to.

ALWAYS REMEMBER TO HAVE CONFIDENCE IN YOUR ABILITIES AND TO ALWAYS REACH FOR THE STARS.

Start with a solid blue painted background and add your two "never"s with a white fine-tip paint pen. Go back in with a black ultra fine-point permanent marker to add "say" to your message and to give the border some fun tangles and your letters some dots. Use turquoise gems to add dots around the edge.

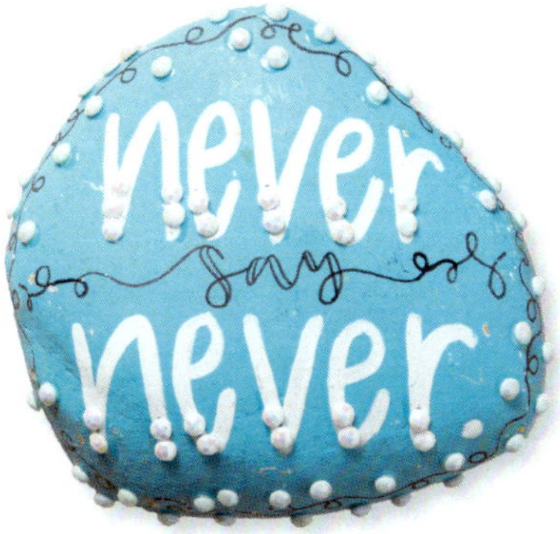

Love ROCKS

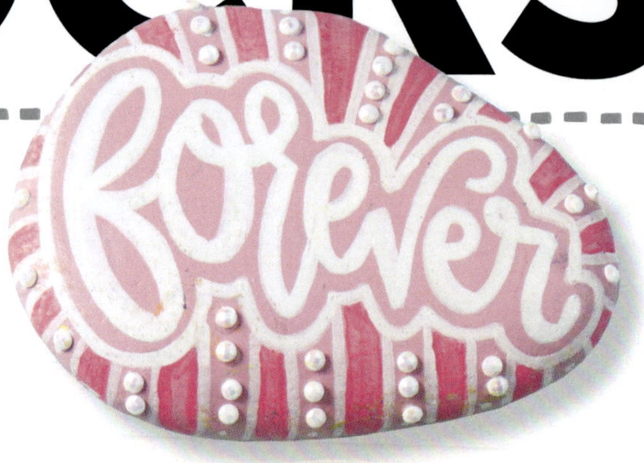

Love, it's what makes . . .

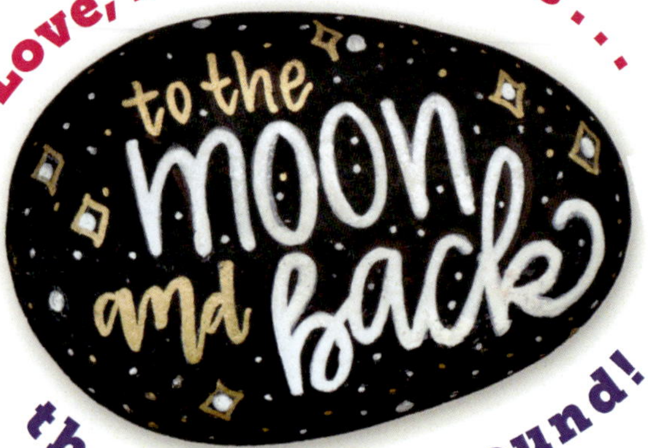

the world go 'round!

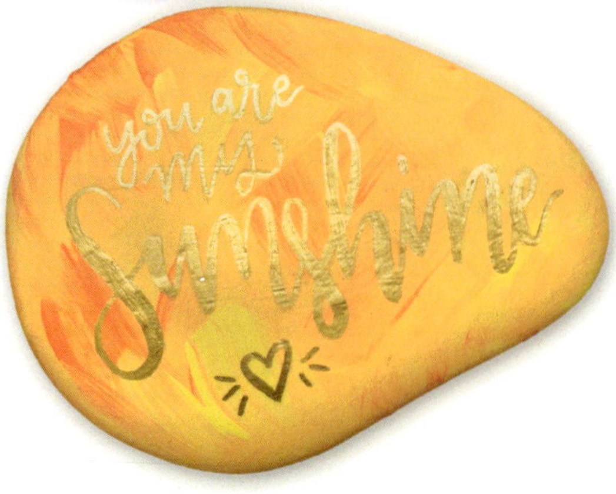

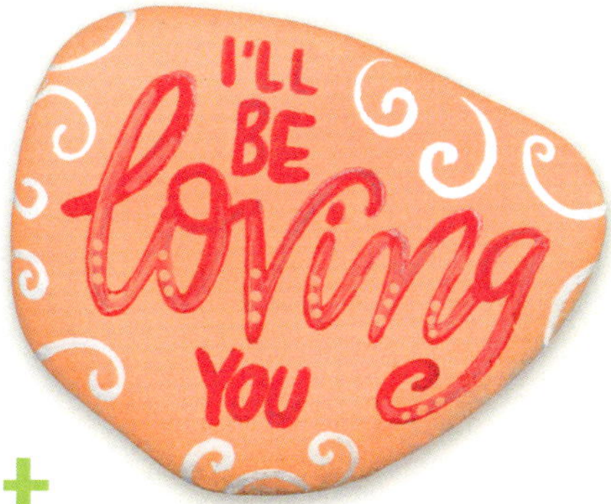

Show the most important **people in your life**

just how much you cherish and appreciate them by painting a memento that will literally withstand the test of time.

In this section you will find six painted rocks that are so full of love, it's amazing it all fits onto one small rock!

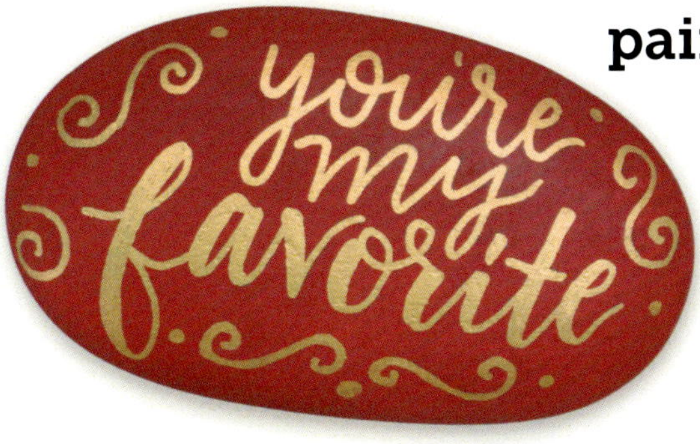

Let's Create the You & Me Rock

What you need

- ☐ the most perfectly round rock you can find
- ☐ acrylic paint (I used red and white.)
- ☐ small and medium synthetic paintbrushes
- ☐ white fine tip paint pen
- ☐ white colored pencil
- ☐ Optional: Diamond Dotz® Gems, Dotz® Stick All Purpose Dotting Adhesive, Dotz® Applicator Tool, and Dotz® Wax

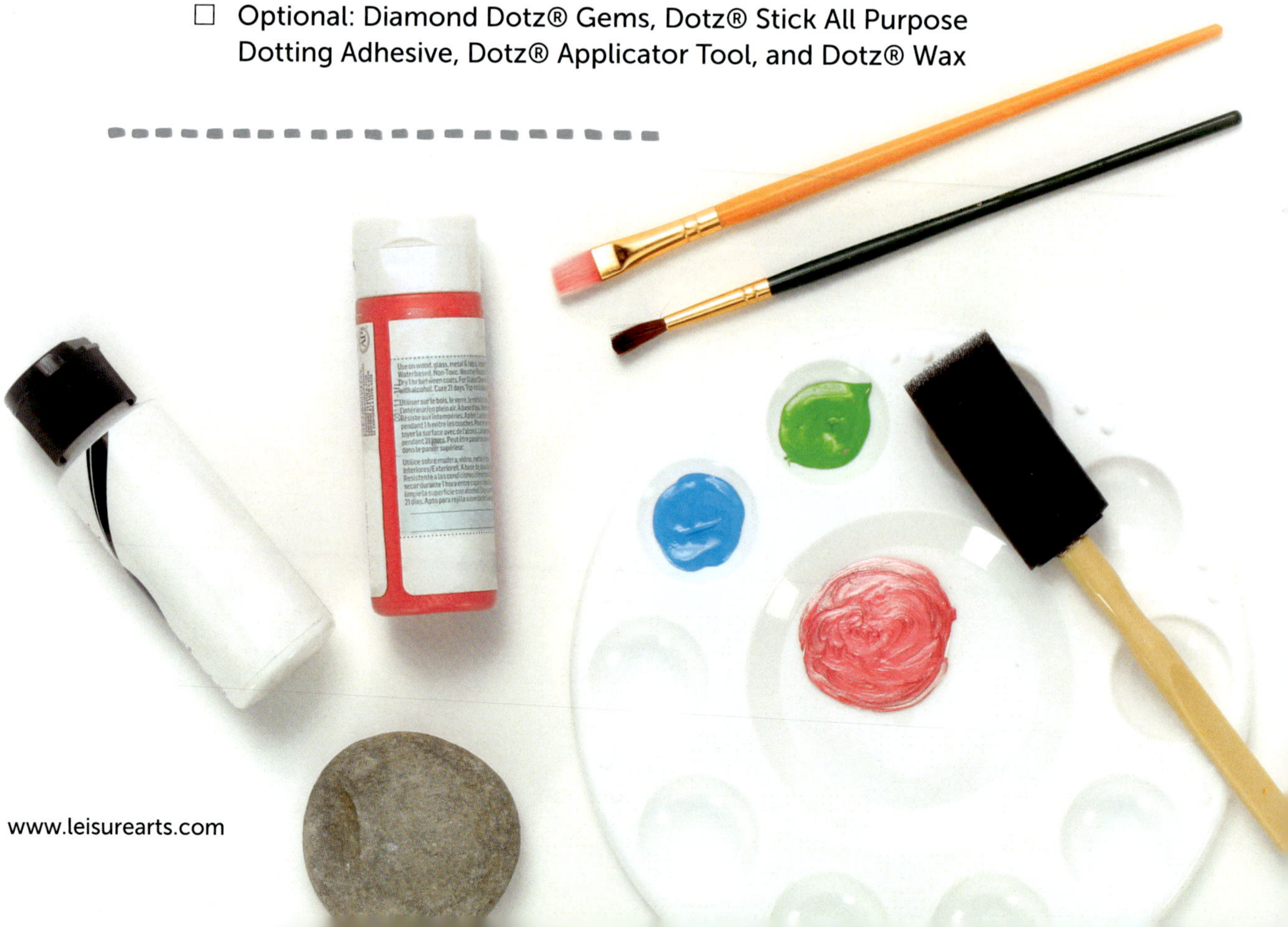

What to do:

1

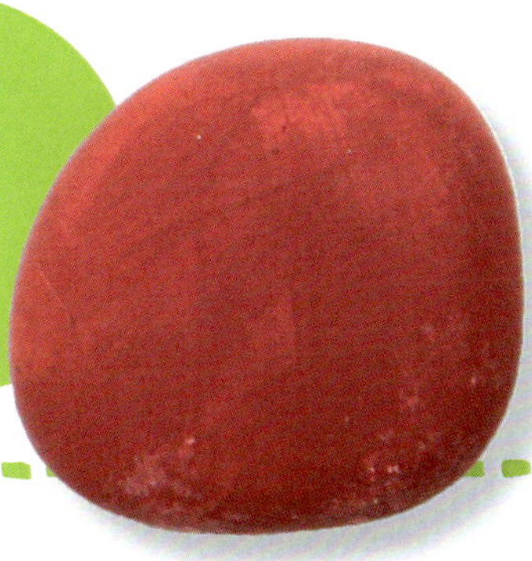

Use the medium paintbrush to paint the rock with two layers of red paint.

2

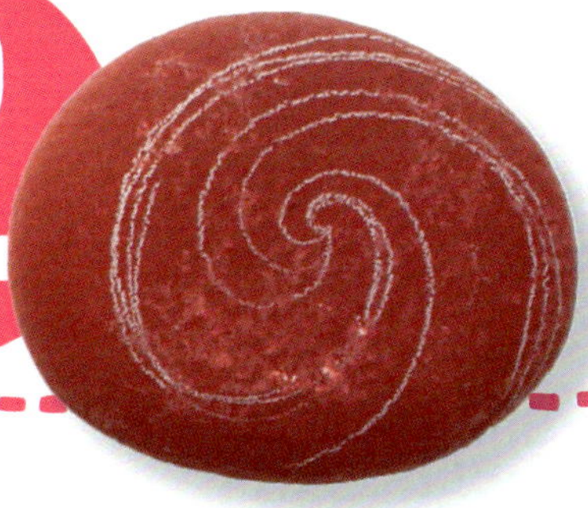

Use the white colored pencil to sketch a spiral pattern starting from the very center of the rock.

3

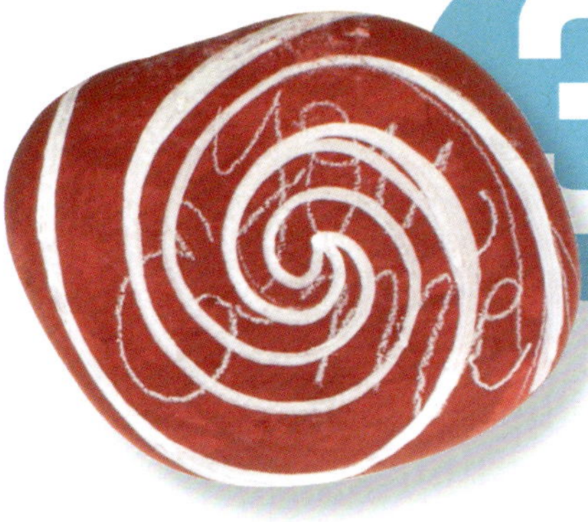

Once you've sketched something you're happy with use the white paint pen to outline the spiral. Use the white colored pencil to sketch the lettering using the FLIRTY ALPHABET. (Try sketching the example ampersand or create your own variation!)

4

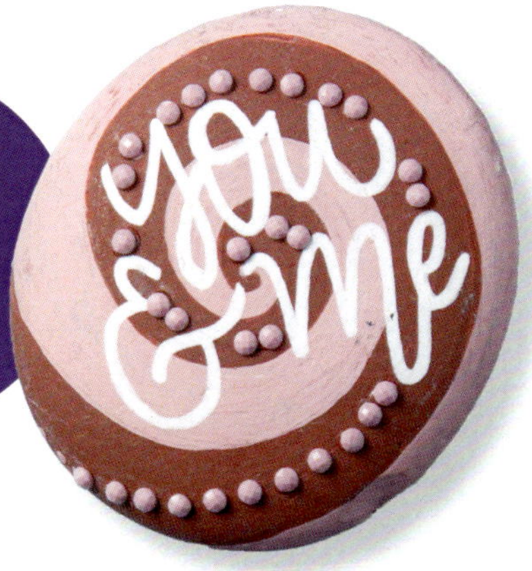

Mix your red paint with a little bit of white to create a pink tone. Use this color and the small paintbrush to paint the spiral. Once your spiral dries, use the paint pen to establish your final lettering. Thicken your letters, perfect your ampersand, and add embellishments to your spiral with your red paint and pink gems.

Be inspired!

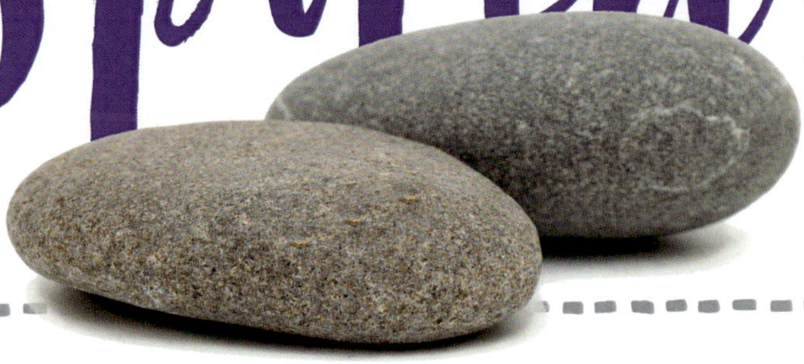

You Are My Sunshine

On even the dreariest of days,

THIS PAINTED PIECE OF SUNSHINE IS SURE TO BRING A SMILE TO YOUR LOVED ONES FACES.

Develop your background by using thick, spontaneous brush strokes of orange and yellow paint to create an abstract painting. Add more than one layer of thick brush strokes to build some texture if you'd like. When dry, use a metallic gold fine tip paint pen to letter your message and heart.

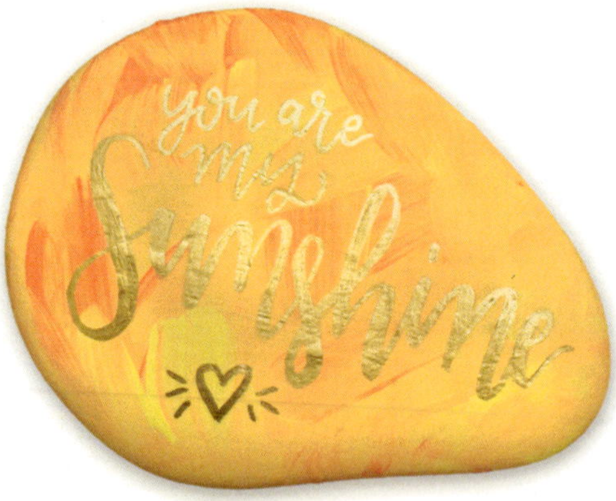

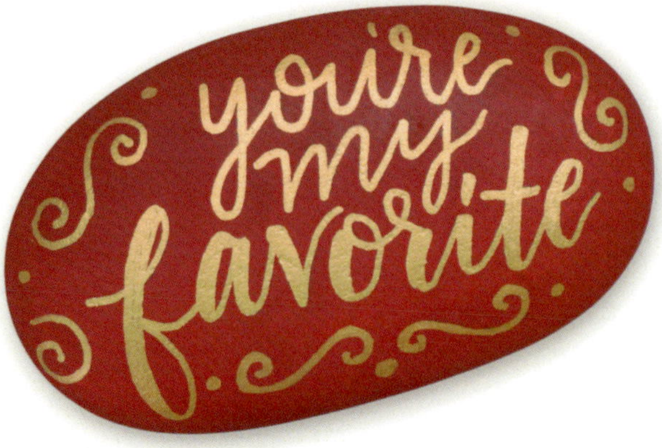

You're My Favorite

This elegant, sweet design is perfect for that one person you just can't get through the day without.

WHETHER A COWORKER, SIGNIFICANT OTHER, OR BEST FRIEND...YOUR FAVORITE PERSON DESERVES TO KNOW JUST HOW MUCH THEIR PRESENCE IN YOUR LIFE MEANS TO YOU!

Apply a thick coat of rich burgundy paint for your background and bring this project to life by using a metallic gold fine tip paint pen for contrast.

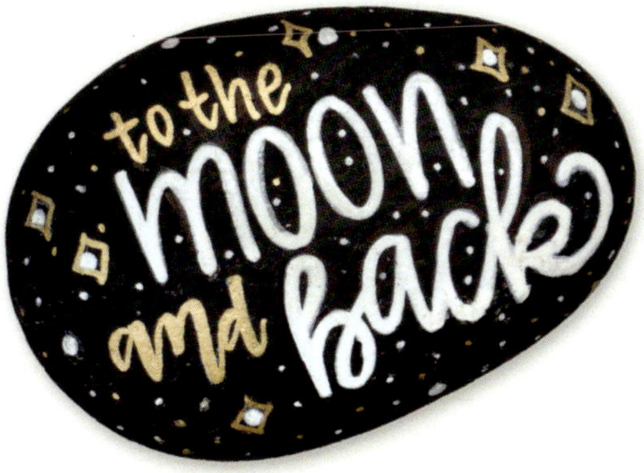

To the Moon and Back

Turn a widely beloved phrase into a lifelong token of love with this beautiful celestial rock project

THAT ANYONE WOULD BE THRILLED TO RECEIVE.

Begin with a crisp black painted background and use bold white paint and a metallic gold fine tip paint pen to make your message stand out like stars in the night sky. Paint white dots outlined in gold paint pen diamonds to further illustrate the idea of stars.

I'll Be Loving You

From now until forever,

MAKE YOUR INTENTIONS KNOWN TO THOSE YOU LOVE WITH THIS PRETTY LITTLE ROCK DESIGN.

Apply a double-layer of coral paint for your background and lay in your script with a small paintbrush and bright magenta paint. Make a slight ombré effect inside the word "loving" by mixing a tiny bit of coral and magenta paint and applying it lightly towards the bottom of the letters, fading upwards. Add white curlicues with a white fine tip paint pen for an extra something special.

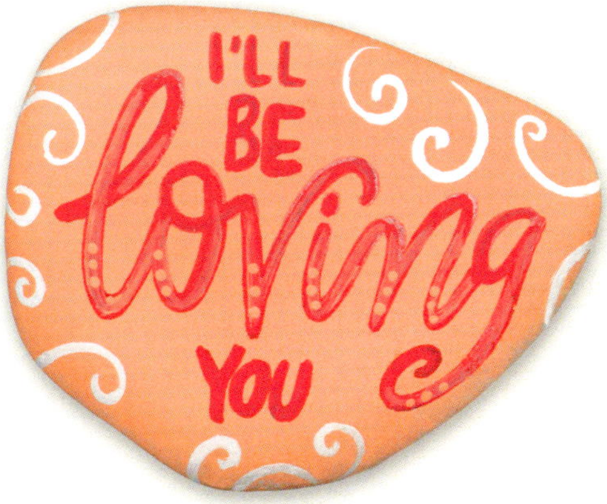

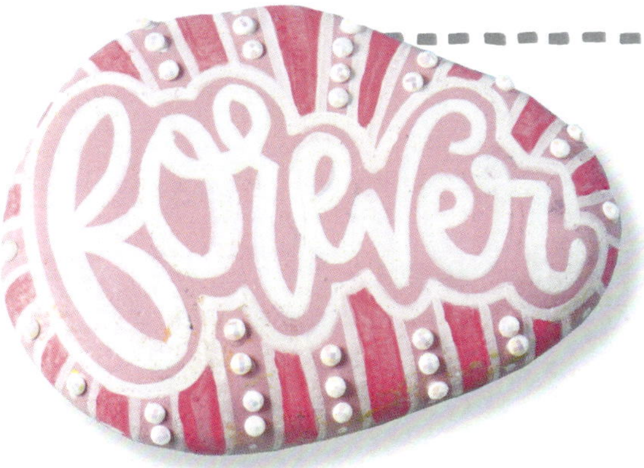

Forever

Let your special someone know just how long you will cherish their love and affection by surprising them with a **"FOREVER" ROCK.**

Use a medium paintbrush to paint your rock pink and use a white fine tip paint pen to lay in your lettering. Add geometric line elements and small dots around your text with a small paintbrush and light pink paint. Paint dark pink backgrounds between the stripes for a little bit of variation. Add gems along the light pink stripes.

Sassy ROCKS

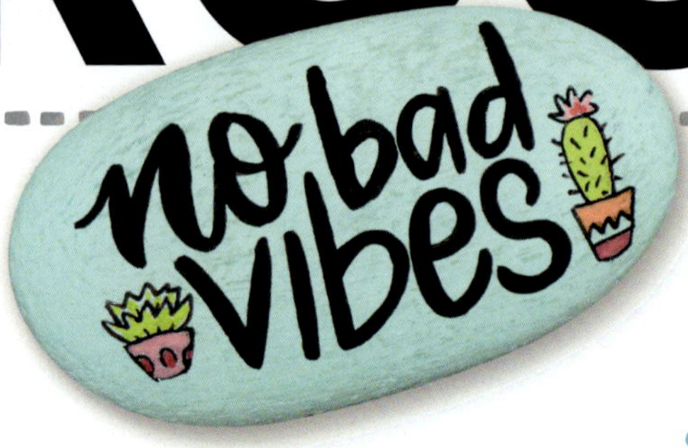

A little sassy, a little sweet . . . that's the attitude that can't be beat!

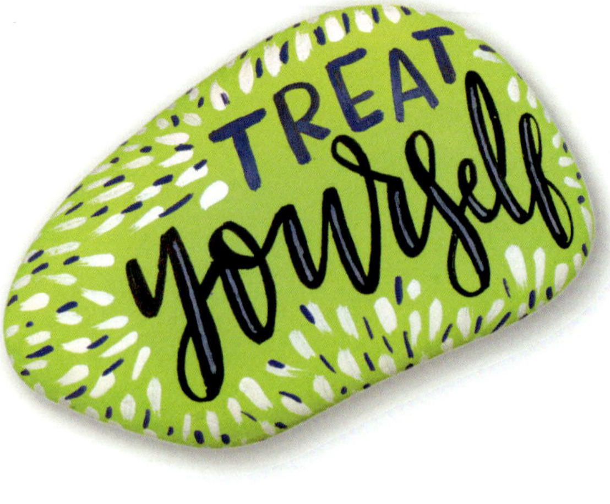

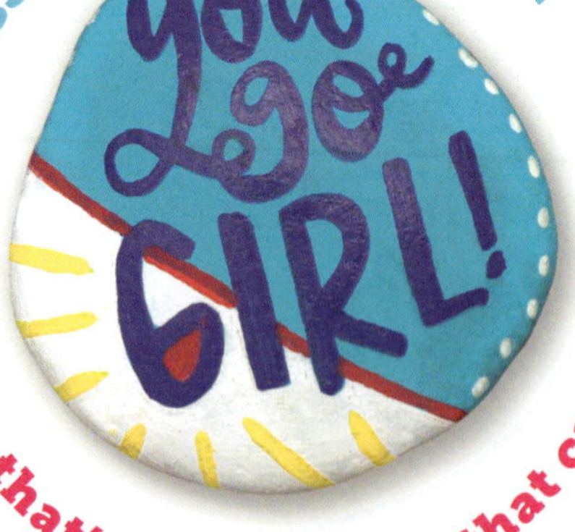

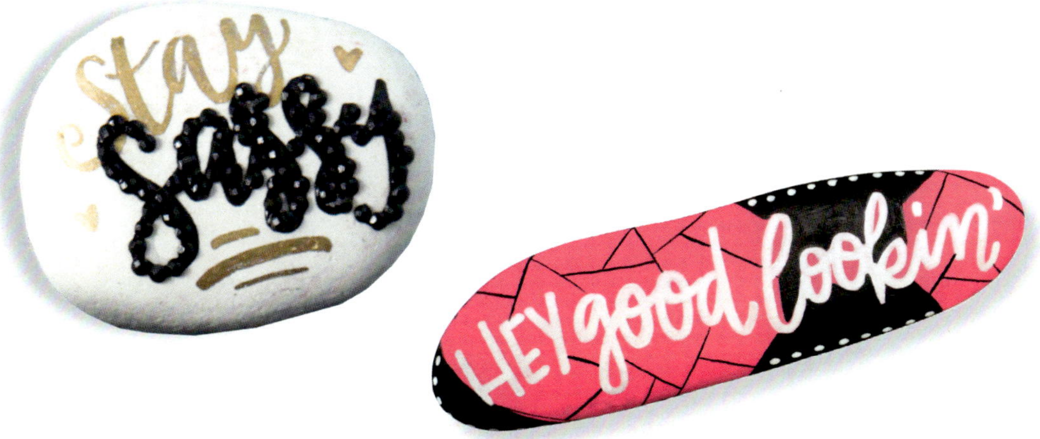

Vibrant colors and no bad vibes,

these designs are sure to bring a smile to your face not only when working on them, but for years after.

Are you a fan of bright colors and bold attitudes? Know someone else who is? If so, the following six painted rock projects were made entirely with you and your friends in mind.

Let's Create the You Rock Rock

What you need:

- rock with an interesting, original shape
- acrylic paint (I used black, pink, turquoise blue, and lime green.)
- small and medium synthetic paintbrushes
- white extra fine tip and fine tip paint pens
- black fine-point permanent marker
- white colored pencil

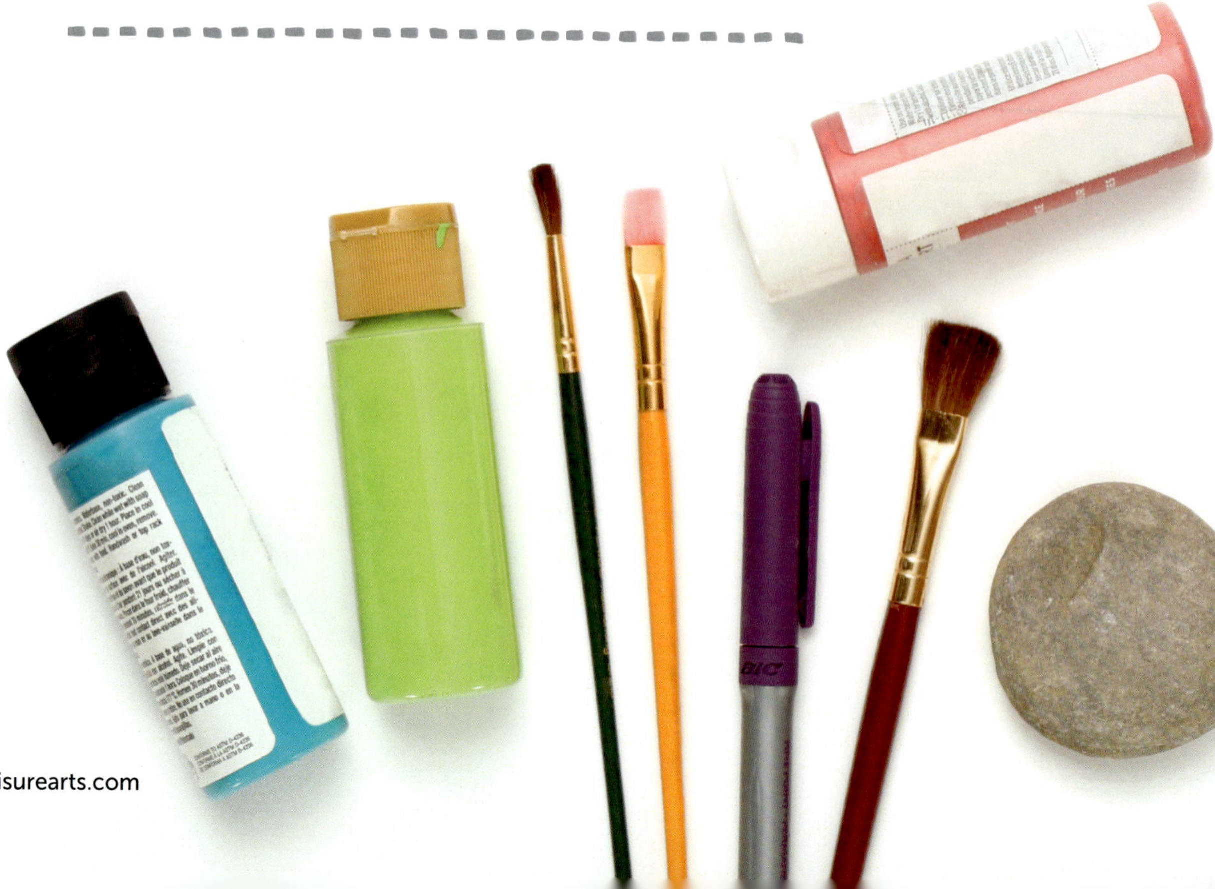

What to do:

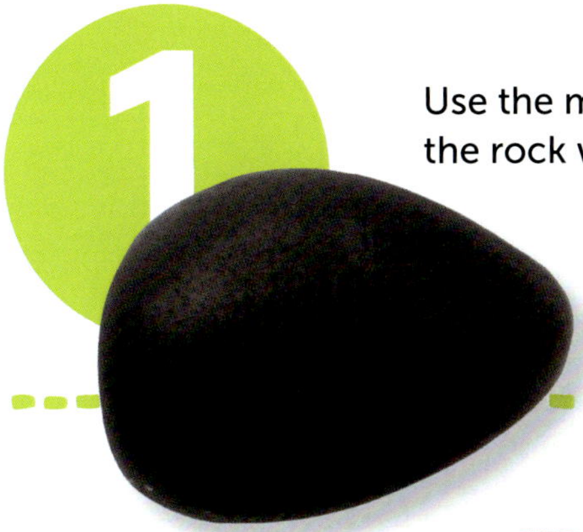

Use the medium paintbrush and black paint to paint the rock with a solid black base coat.

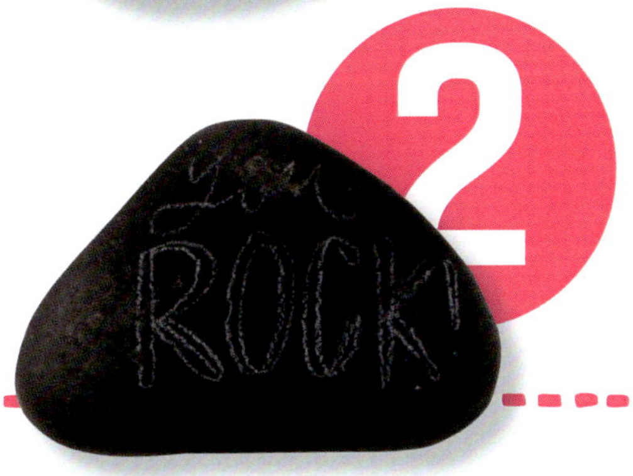

Use the white colored pencil to sketch out your lettering using the MODERN and FLIRTY ALPHABETS as a guide.

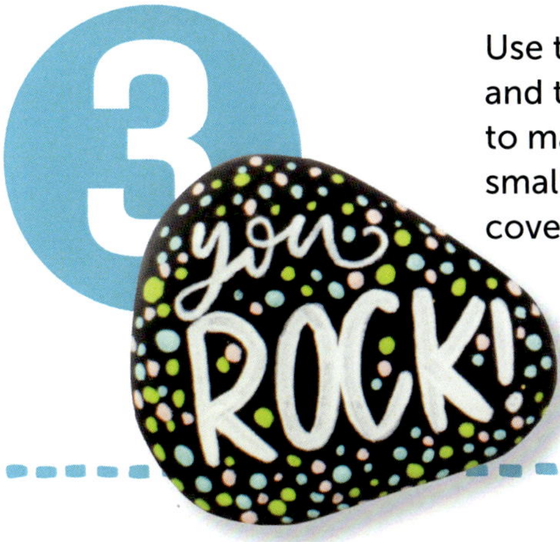

Use the white extra fine tip paint pen to outline "you" and the white fine tip paint pen (which is a little thicker) to make "rock!" bolder. With the small paintbrush, make small dots in pink, turquoise blue, and lime green to cover the entire black background.

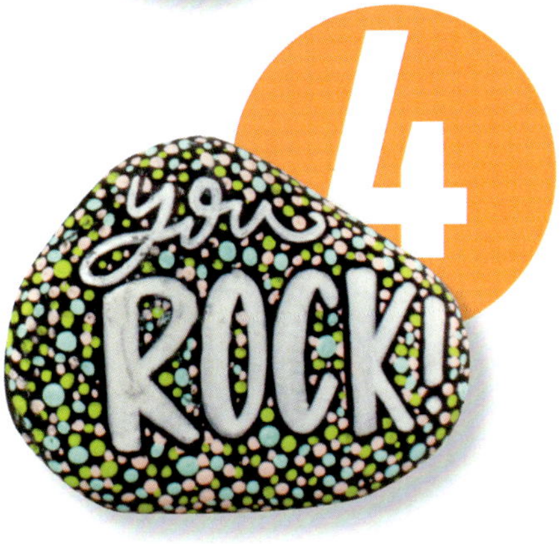

After your dots have dried, use a black permanent marker to outline "you" and "rock!" so the letters stand out a little better.

Be inspired!

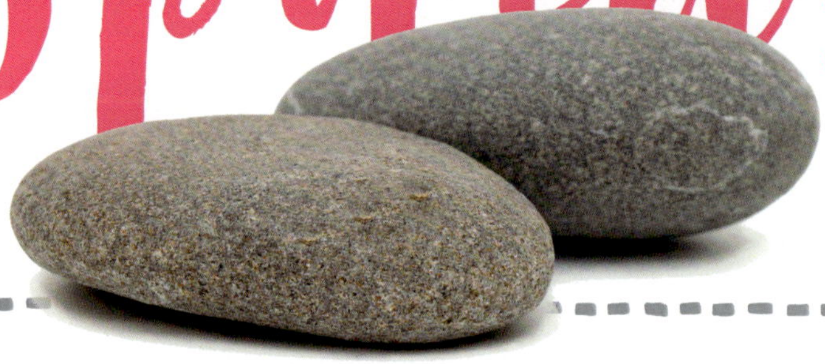

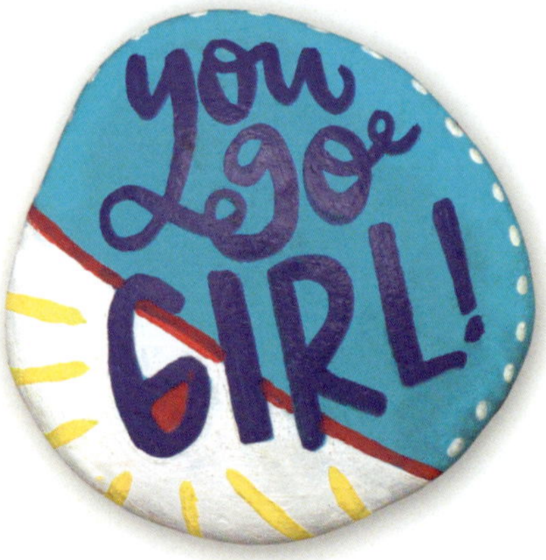

You Go Girl!

Need some motivation to be your best "go get 'em, girl!" self?

THIS COLORFUL PROJECT WILL PUT SOME PEP IN YOUR STEP ON YOUR WAY OUT THE DOOR IN THE MORNING.

Paint $^{2}/_{3}$ of your rock bright blue, and the remaining section white. Then, use bright pink paint to add some pops of contrast amid white and yellow painted doodles. Finally, use a fine tip paint pen to add rich purple lettering for a really funky look!

No Bad Vibes

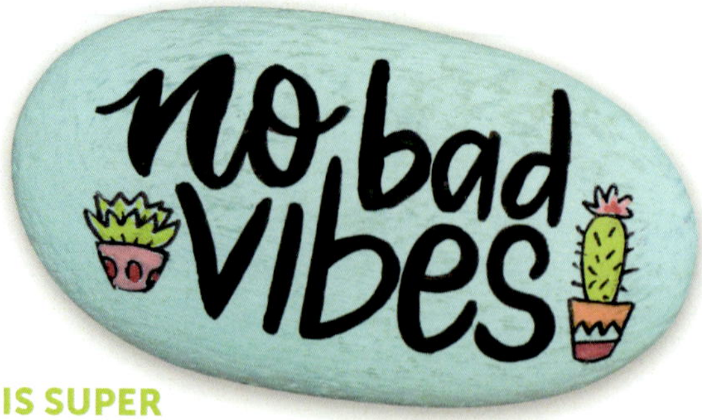

Simple, direct, and to the point: no bad vibes here!

KICK THOSE NEGATIVE THOUGHTS TO THE CURB BY TRYING THIS SUPER TRENDY, ADORABLE ROCK PROJECT.

Lay down an aqua paint background. Use a small paintbrush and black paint to add thick black text that incorporates 2 different lettering styles. Don't be intimidated by the cacti… they're just simple doodles! Draw your succulent friends with a black fine-point permanent marker and carefully add a little bit of color with paint and a tiny paintbrush.

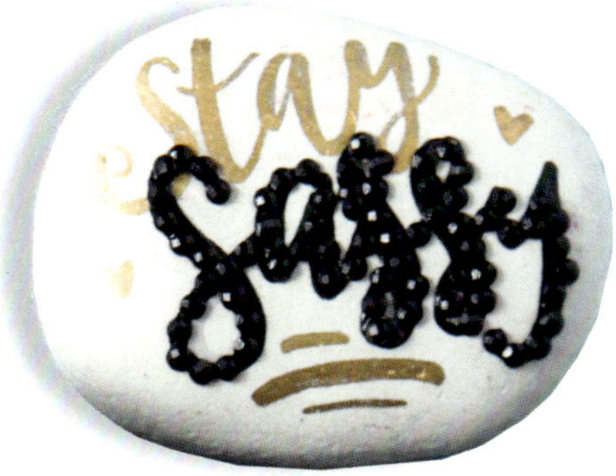

Stay Sassy

OBEY THE ROCK:

always stay sassy and never compromise your sense of self... even if that sense of self has a little bit of an attitude!

Apply a healthy coating of white paint for your base and then use black and metallic gold fine tip paint pens to add some extra sweet lettering (with little hearts for good measure). Make your lettering shine by adding a line of gems over a word.

Hey Good Lookin'

This one is dedicated to the super sassy,

TOUGH-AS-NAILS GIRL WE ALL HAVE DEEP DOWN INSIDE OF US.

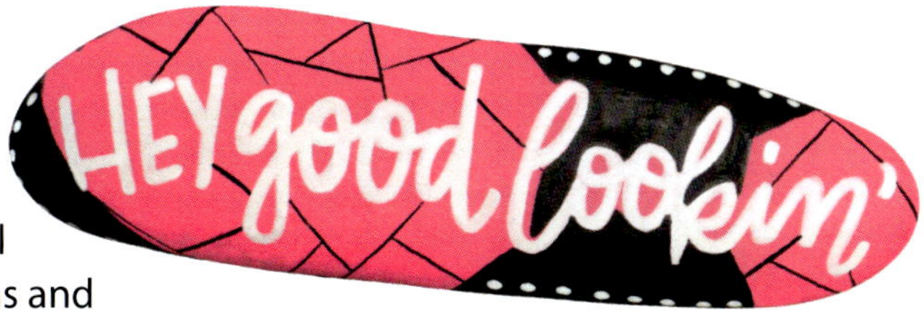

Start with a hot, hot, hot pink painted background and add your text with a white fine tip paint pen. Create some geometric sections around your lettering with a small paintbrush and black paint. Embellish with thin black prisms and white dots created with a black fine-point permanent marker and white fine tip paint pen.

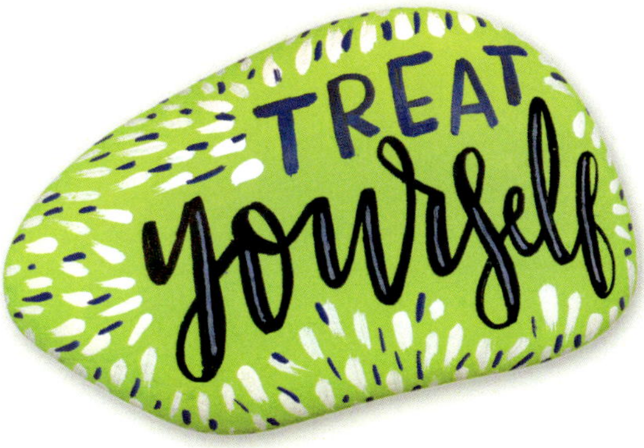

Treat Yourself

ONE OF THE MOST IMPORTANT LIFE-LESSONS OF ALL:

don't forget to take care of yourself every once in a while. You work so hard...why not give yourself some credit and treat yourself to something special.

A bright green painted background, black and purple fine tip paint pen text, and a feathery white paint and black paint pen design will leave you with a really unique project. Try using a white fine tip paint pen to add some dimension lines to the inside of your lettering for some extra flair.

Faith ROCKS

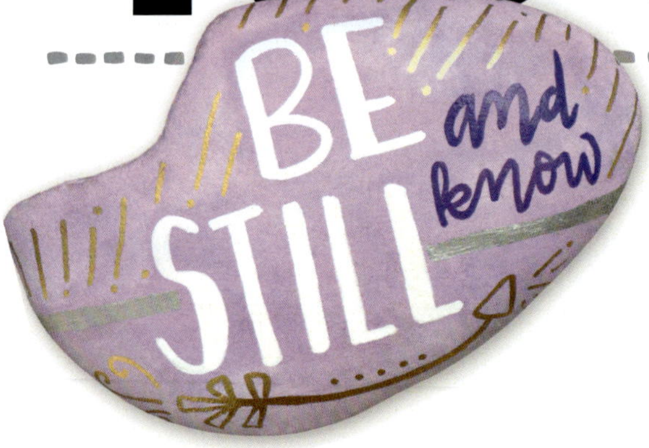

Try to be a rainbow . . .

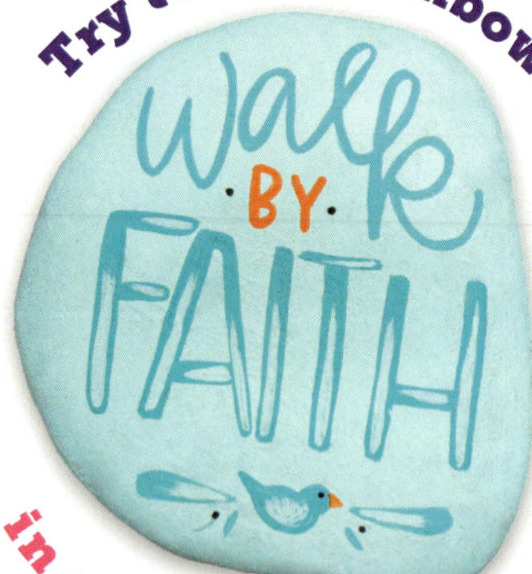

in someone's cloud.

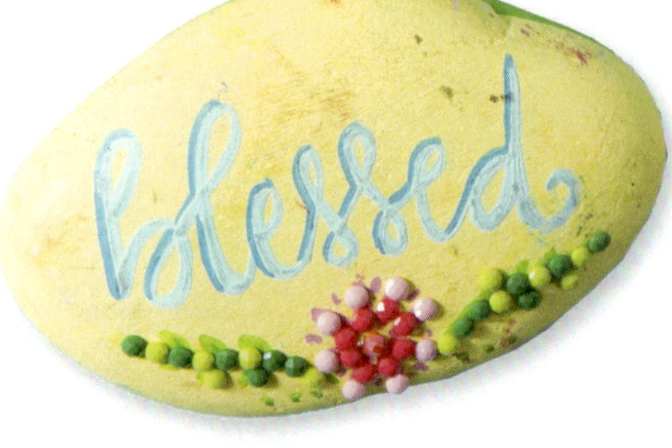

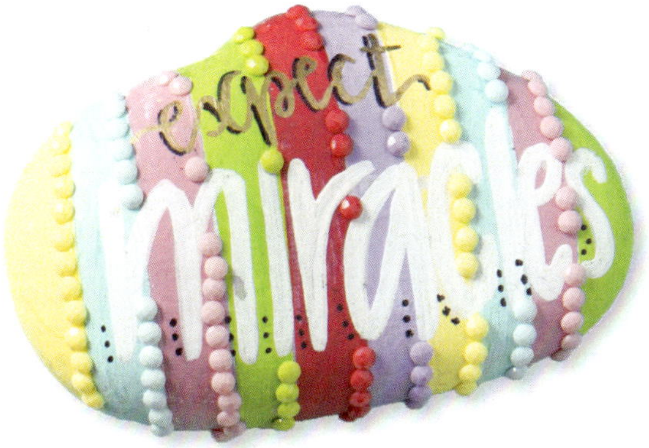

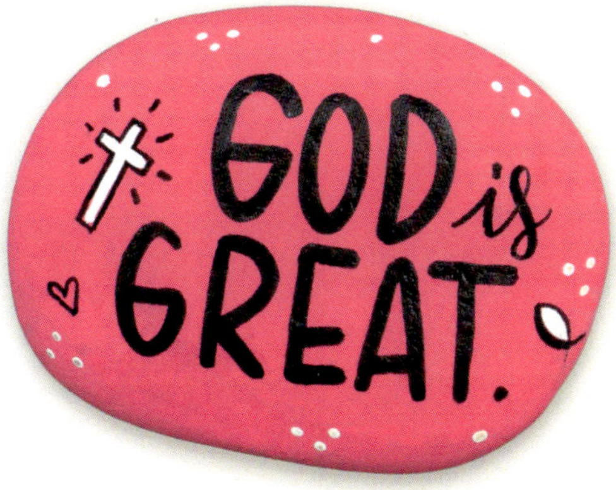

We all know that

the world we live in

can be a scary and intimidating place sometimes, a place full of doubt and uncertainty;

however, if we hold our heads high and always hang on to our faith, anything that life throws at us is something we can handle! In this section, you'll find six designs that can inspire love and faith in you and your loved ones, both young and old.

Let's Create the Grace Rock

What you need:

- ☐ rounded, evenly shaped rock
- ☐ acrylic paint (I used white and turquoise blue.)
- ☐ small and medium synthetic paintbrushes
- ☐ silver fine tip paint pen
- ☐ #2 lead pencil or dark colored pencil

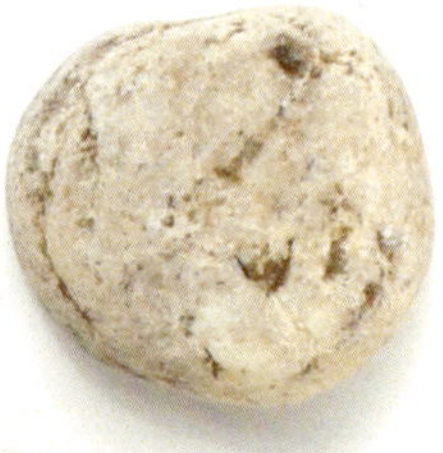

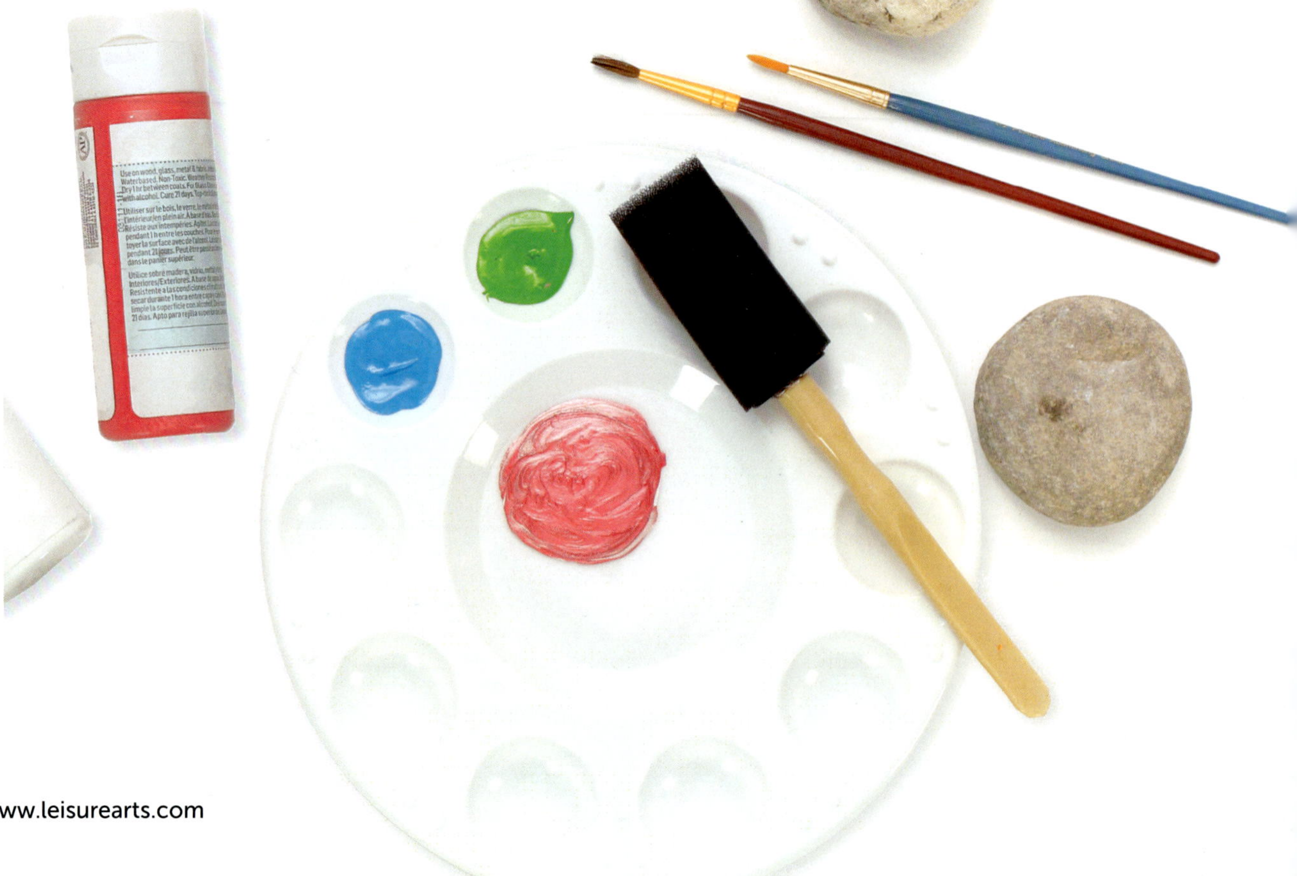

What to do:

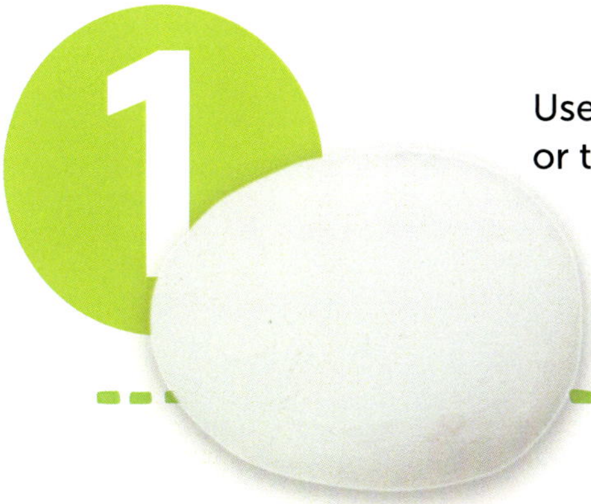

Use the medium paintbrush to paint two or three layers of solid white paint.

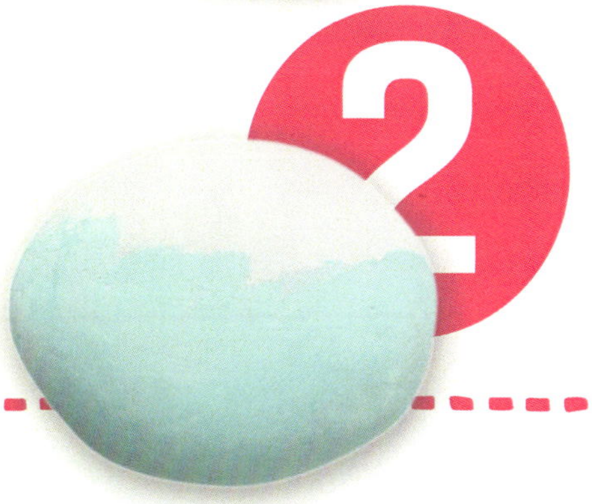

Using your turquoise blue paint, cover the bottom half of your rock, allowing the paint to fade lightly as you reach the center.

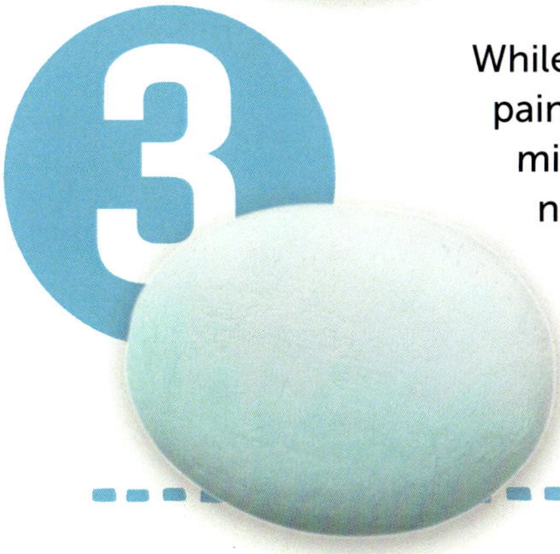

While your turquoise blue paint is still wet, apply more white paint from the top, fading down... the two will merge in the middle to create an ombré effect. You may need to apply numerous coats of both colors, mixing in the middle, to achieve a nice blend. (Try practicing on a spare rock or piece of paper if you haven't done this technique before!)

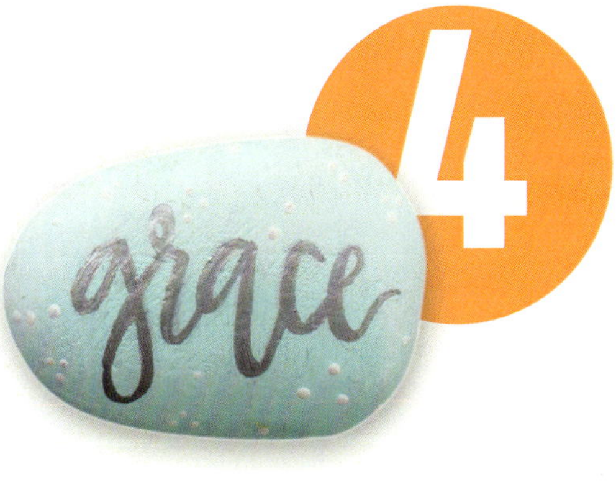

Using the CLASSIC ALPHABET, sketch the lettering with a #2 lead pencil or dark colored pencil. Outline your sketch of "grace" with a metallic silver fine tip paint pen and add small white dot/star embellishments using the small paintbrush and white paint.

Be *inspired!*

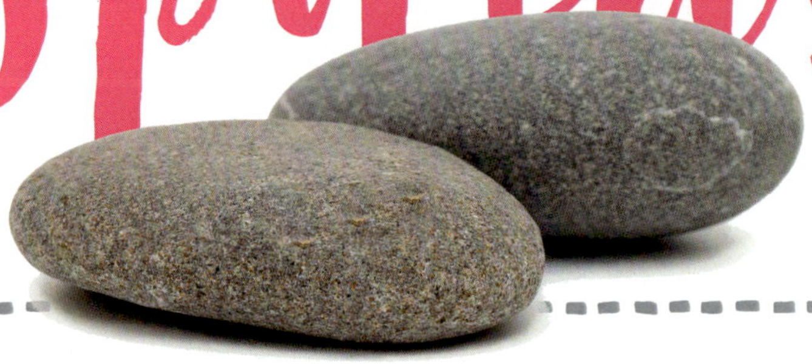

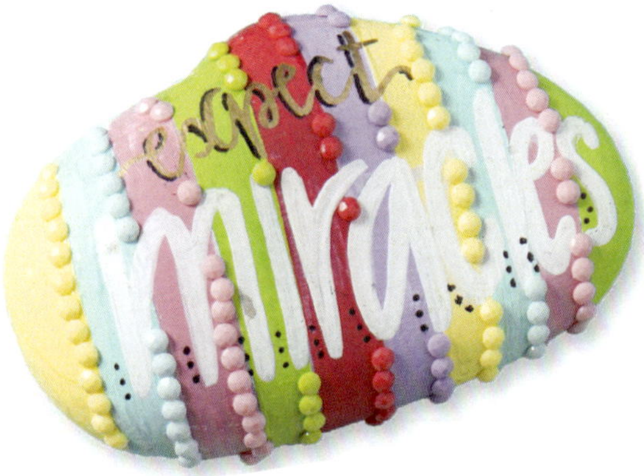

EXPECT MIRACLES

These bright stripes of yellow, blue, pink, green, magenta, and purple urge you to expect the unexpected,

AND TO ALWAYS EXPECT MIRACLES TO HAPPEN!

Freehand your stripes or use small strips of tape to paint straight lines, then add thick white text and delicate gold lettering with your fine tip paint pens. After your paint has dried, add black dots and drop shadows with black fine-point permanent marker for extra detailing. Add colorful gems along each stripe.

BE STILL AND KNOW

When you feel rushed and vulnerable,

TAKE A MOMENT TO BE STILL AND KNOW.

Paint a basecoat of pretty lavender and letter your words with white and purple fine tip paint pens (draw in pencil first if you're not sure of placement). When finished lettering, add gold and silver ribbons and a whimsical arrow design with metallic fine tip paint pens.

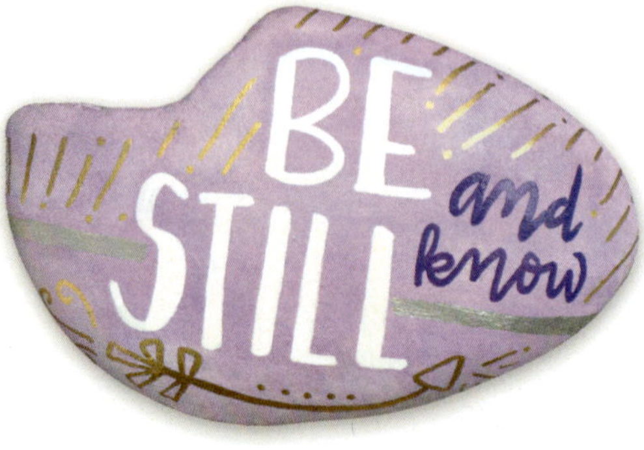

GOD IS GREAT

VIBRANT AND UNDENIABLE, JUST LIKE GOD'S LOVE,

this design is easy to achieve and leaves you with a very dynamic final product.

A hot pink painted background with thick block lettering in black fine tip paint pen makes the sentiment really stand out. Add some doodling and embellishment dots with your black fine-point permanent marker and a white fine tip paint pen for a simply cute and modern project.

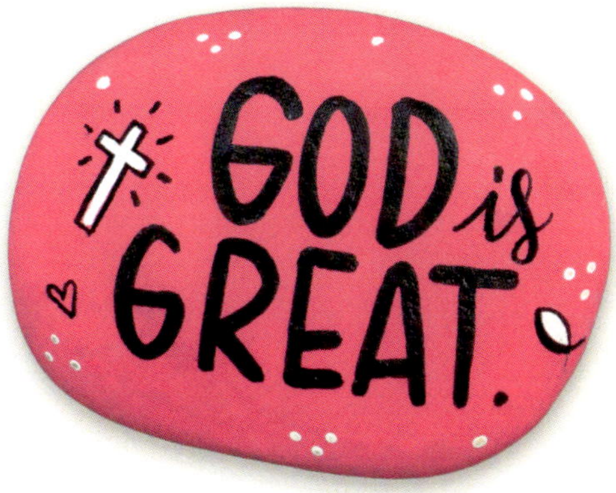

BLESSED

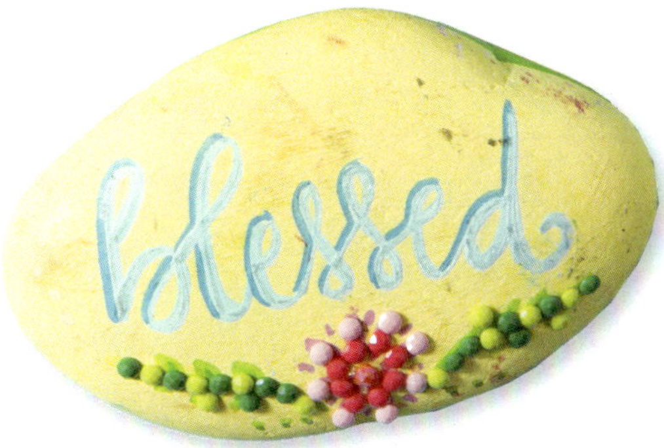

REMIND YOURSELF EVERYDAY HOW TRULY BLESSED YOU ARE

with this delicate, beautiful project.

Start with a creamy yellow painted basecoat and add your lettering with a small paintbrush and light blue paint. Paint a pink flower with extended green leaves below your text. Paint special details like drop shadows on the lettering and elements of shading within the flower and leaves to add dimension. Embellish the flower and leaves with gems.

WALK BY FAITH

SOMETIMES WE VENTURE DOWN PATHS IN LIFE THAT HAVE UNKNOWN DESTINATIONS,

but if we walk by faith we will always find our way. This pretty sentiment is perfectly illustrated with cool shades of blue and hints of warm orange paints.

Paint a little bird at the bottom (practice your doodles on page 17 first if you want!) and add some light blue to your darker lettering and black permanent pen dots for a fun effect.

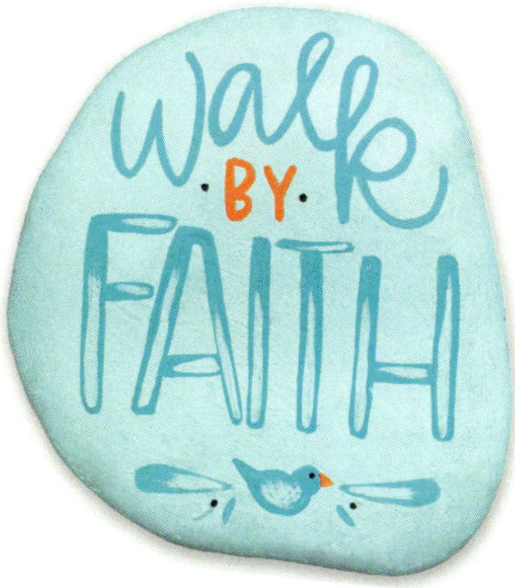

Motivation ROCKS

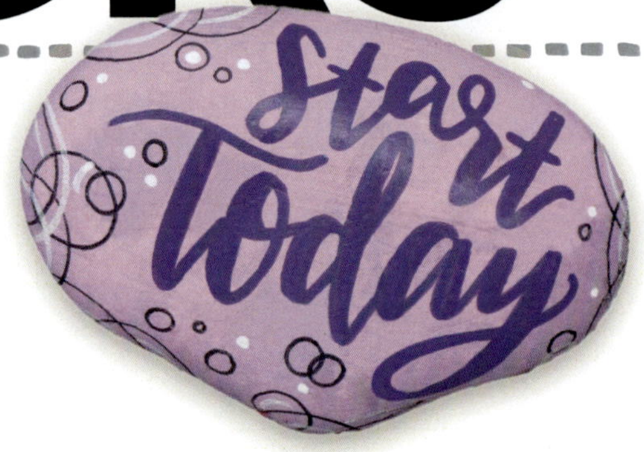

Don't count the days . . .

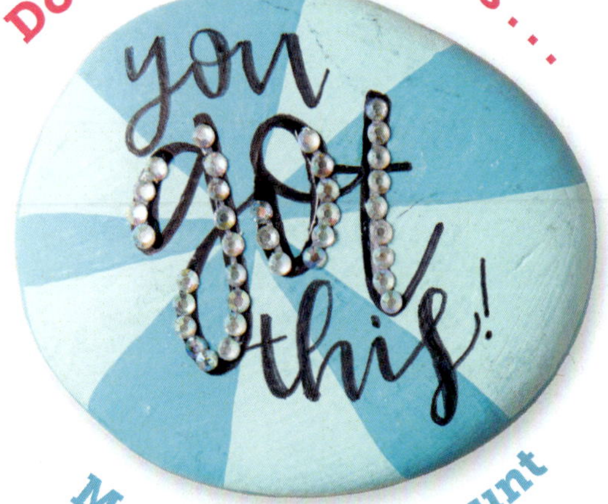

Make the days count

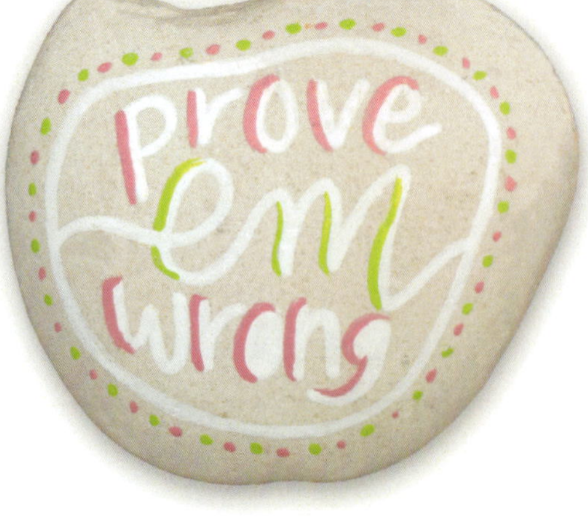

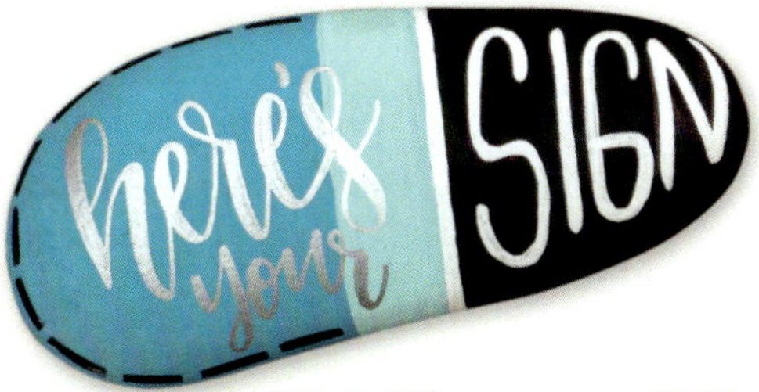

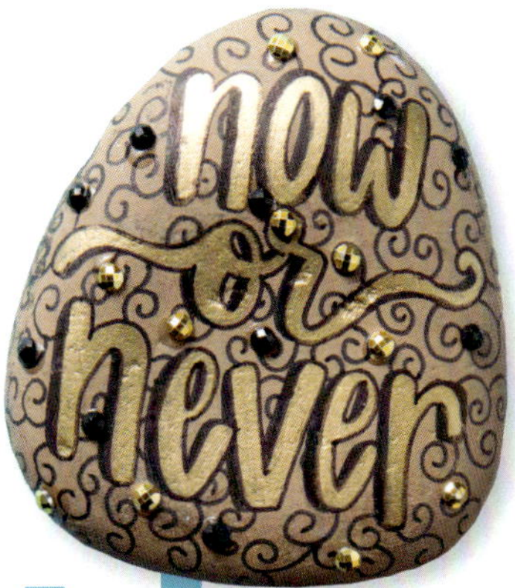

We all know how hard it is

to keep ourselves on track with our goals and dreams, right? Some days, just getting out of bed to face the trials and tribulations of our day-to-day lives feels like the biggest chore in the universe.

The six rock designs you will find in this section can serve as your little cheerleaders... on your nightstand, in your car, or on your work desk. Just a daily reminder that "you got this!"

Let's Create the Make your Mark Rock

What you need:

- ☐ large, flat-bottomed rock
- ☐ acrylic paint (I used pink, light pink, green, and white.)
- ☐ small and medium synthetic paintbrushes
- ☐ green fine tip paint pen
- ☐ black fine-point permanent marker
- ☐ #2 lead pencil or dark colored pencil

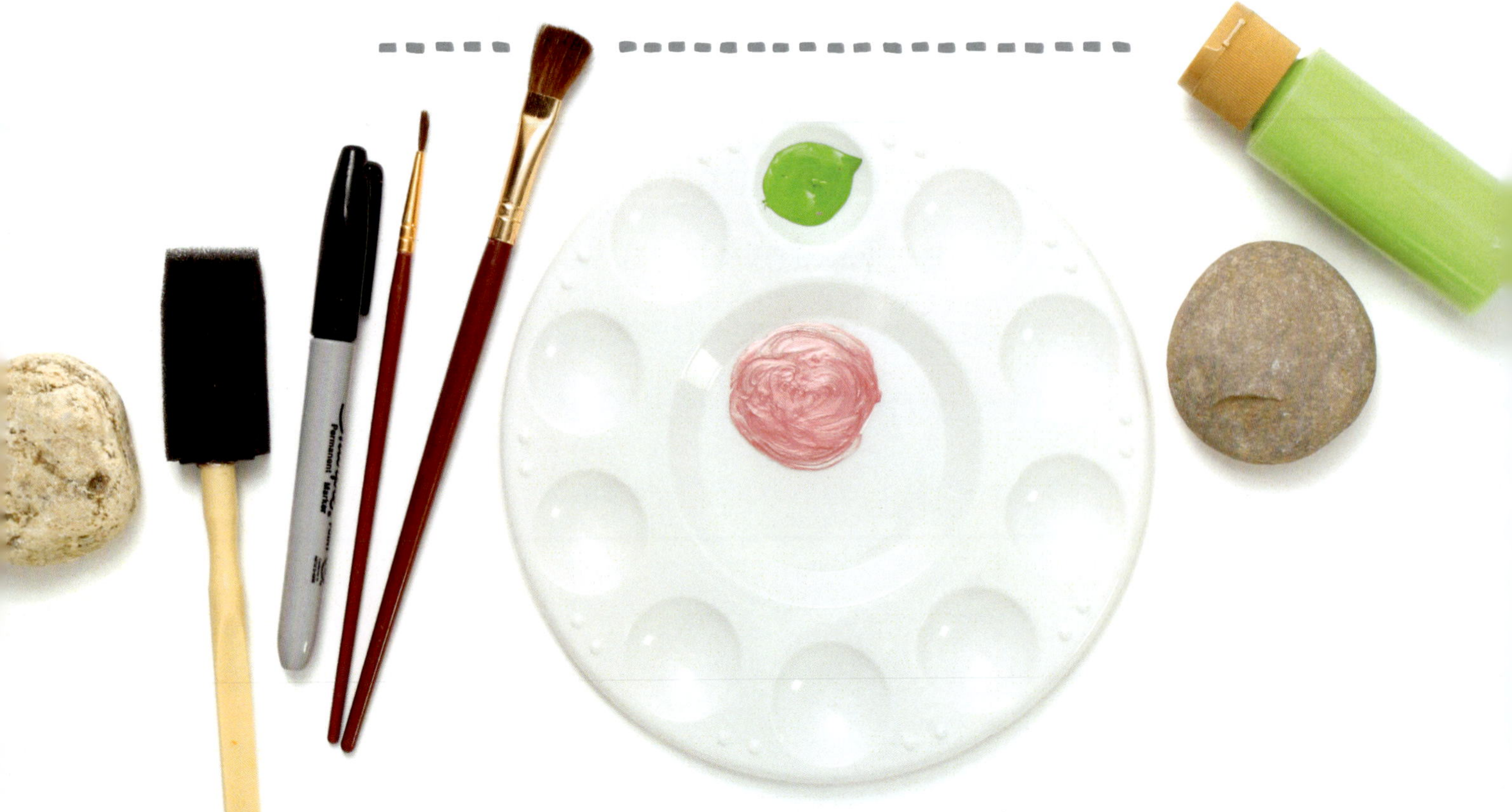

What to do:

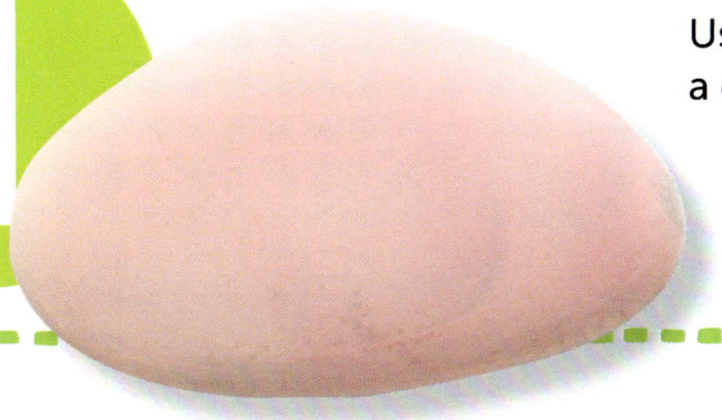

1. Use the medium paintbrush to paint a double-layer basecoat of light pink.

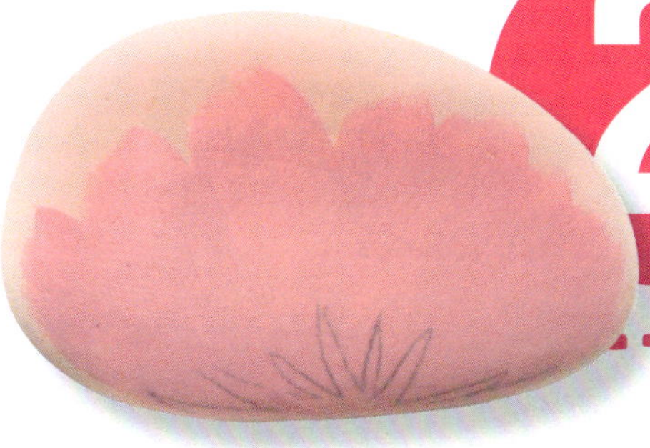

2. Once the basecoat has dried, use the medium paintbrush and pink paint to create loose petal-like shapes. Then use the lead pencil or dark colored pencil to begin the outline of the flower's base at the bottom of the rock.

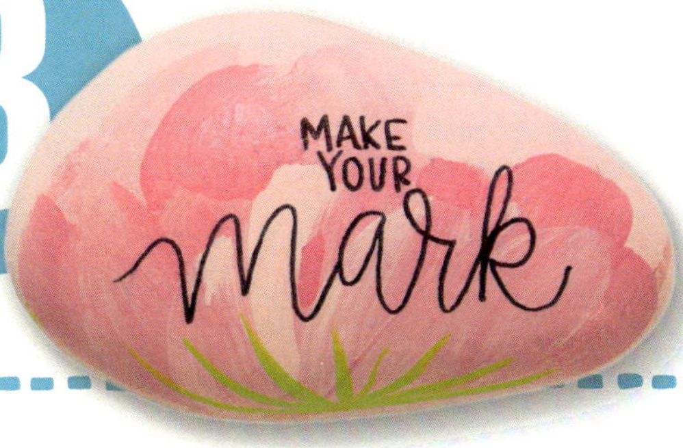

3. Use your white, light pink, and pink paints to add some dimension to the petals of your flower. Keep the lighter colors towards the base of the flower and darker tones towards the outside of the petals. Fill in the green base with green paint. Use the permanent marker and your MODERN and CLASSIC ALPHABETS to sketch your lettering.

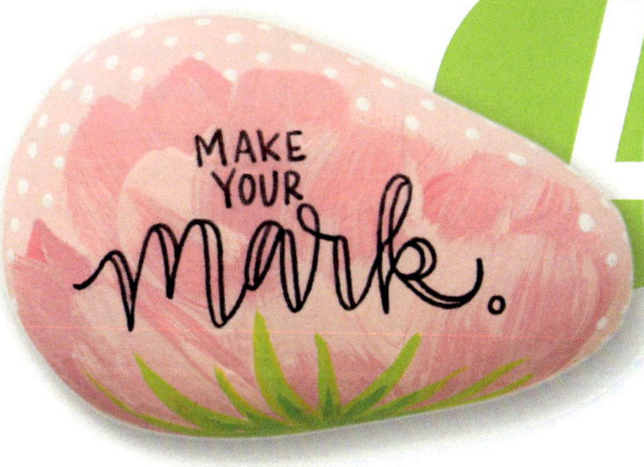

4. Once you're happy with your flower petals and lettering position, add small white dots to the background with your small paintbrush. Finally, outline your lettering with the black permanent marker.

Be inspired!

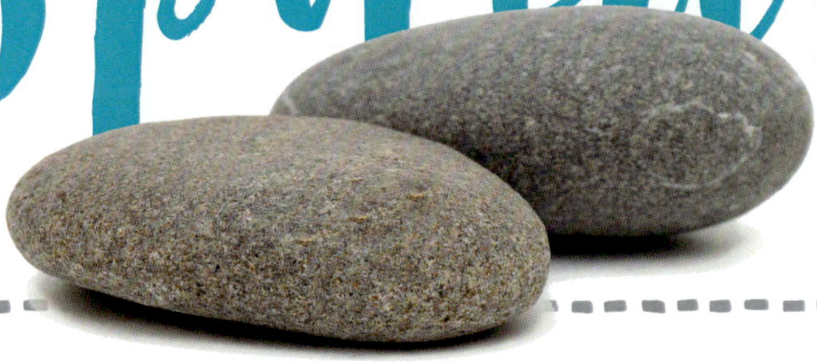

Start Today

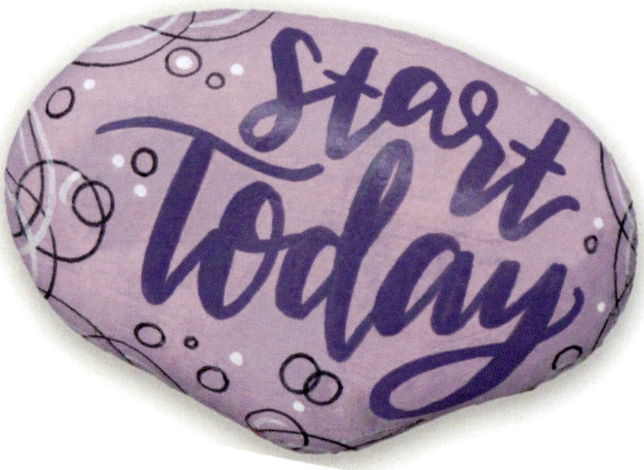

WHAT BETTER DAY TO START THAN TODAY?

That new hobby you want to try, that lifestyle change you want to make: you are capable of achieving anything you put your mind to... and there's no time like the present!

Create this bubbly project by painting a light purple background, using a dark purple fine tip paint pen for your lettering, and creating interlacing circle doodles with a white fine tip paint pen and a black fine-point permanent marker.

Here's Your Sign

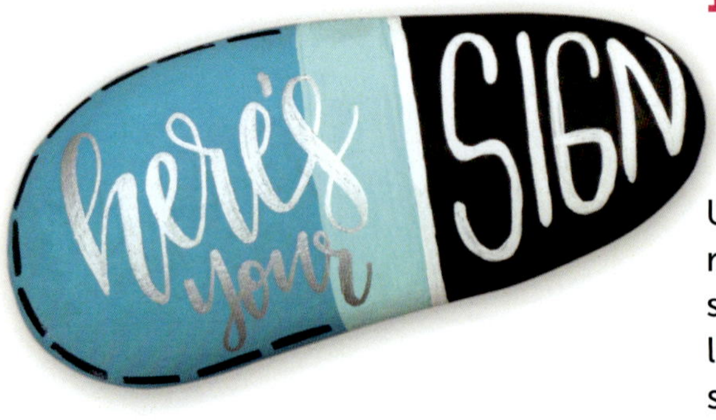

This sleek, geometric project is telling you to go with your gut instinct and to **FOLLOW YOUR HEART**...this is your sign!

Using light aqua, turquoise, and black paint, split your rock into thirds and paint accordingly. Use metallic silver and white fine tip paint pens to apply your lettering, then paint a black stitch design around one side and a solid white line through the middle.

Prove 'em Wrong

On the days when it feels like no one has much faith in your abilities: just prove 'em wrong! Your boss, your parents, your friends, your peers...

PUT ON A BRAVE FACE AND SHOW THEM ALL HOW STRONG YOU ARE.

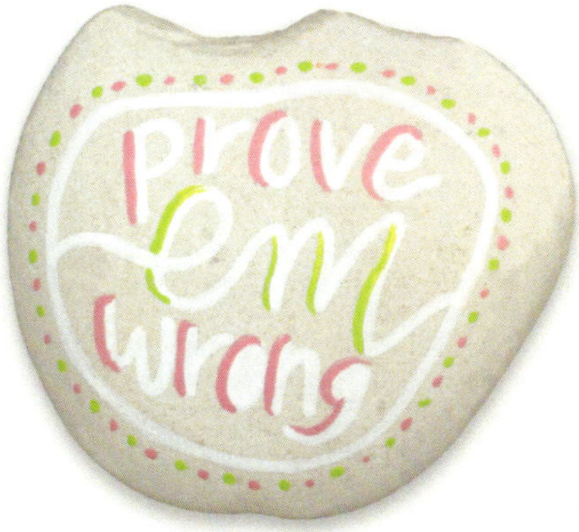

For this project, keep your rock unpainted and draw a circle with white fine tip paint pen that follows the organic shape of the rock you're using (make sure to leave plenty of space for your lettering). Add your lettering with white paint pen, then paint pink and green drop shadows and alternating dots around the outside of the circle.

You Got This

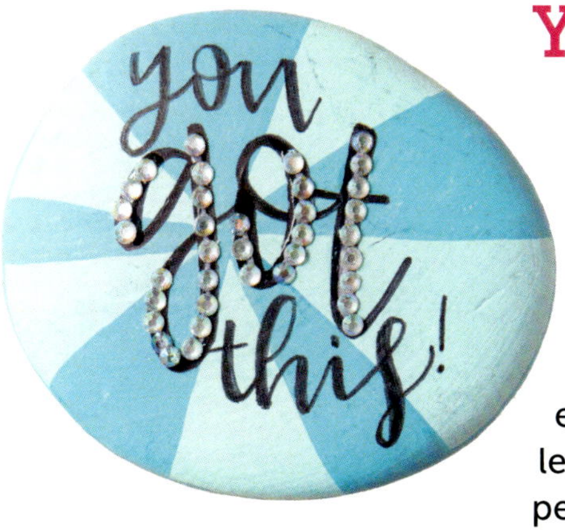

When you need reassurance, look at this pretty pinwheel and rest assured that no matter what the day throws at you,

YOU CAN HANDLE IT.

Paint the entire face of your rock with aqua and then, when dry, add in pinwheel sections in turquoise (it's much easier than it looks and you really can't screw it up!). Draw your lettering over the center of the pinwheel in black fine tip paint pen and add sparkly gems to the word for a little dimension.

Now or Never

If you're the type of person who procrastinates or can never seem to make up their mind when it comes to a plan, this project is for you!

SOMETIMES A "NOW OR NEVER" APPROACH IS WHAT WE NEED TO MOTIVATE US AND THIS IS YOUR REMINDER TO GET GOING.

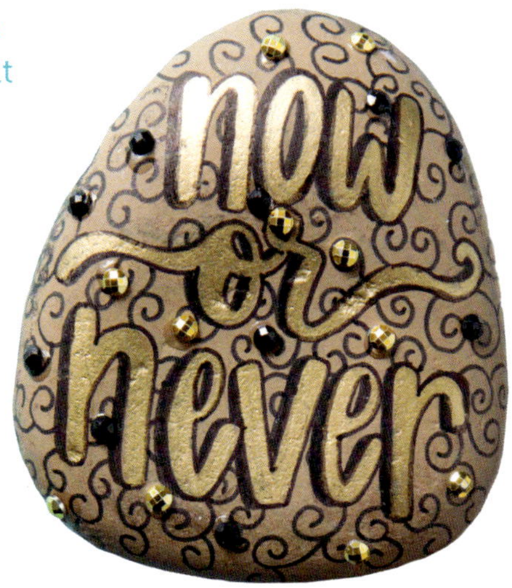

Paint your rock light brown, and then add thick lettering in metallic gold fine tip paint pen. When dry, outline your text and add thick drop shadows with a black fine-point permanent marker; finish this elegant project by adding thin curlicues and a spattering of gold and black gems all over the background.

Meet Kati Erney

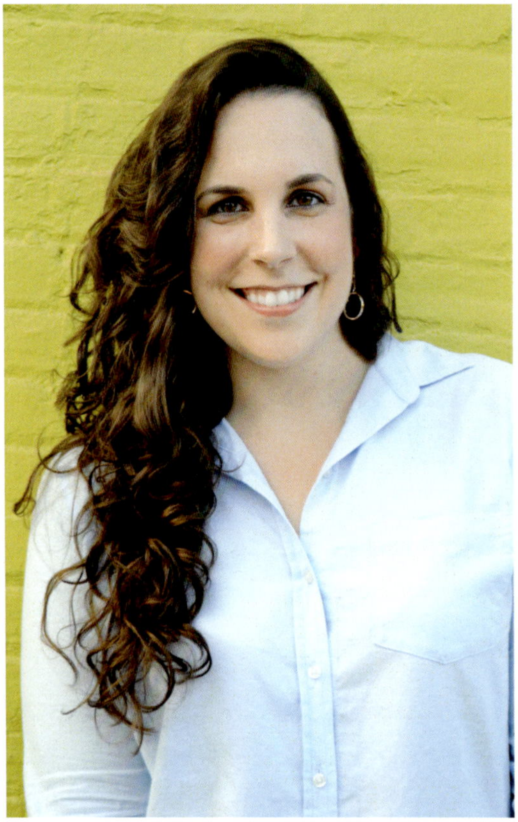

Look for other Leisure Arts books featuring Kati's designs at www.leisurearts.com/meet-the-designers/kathryn-erney.html

Kathryn Erney is a self-taught (and still learning!) hand lettering artist and lover of all things crafty and creative. Born and raised in Central Pennsylvania, Kati's passions in life have always planted roots in the arts and in nature. From an initial educational interest in fine art, graphic design, and art history, her recent experience in the trend-setting world of craft book publishing has led her to new, blossoming success in the realm of adult coloring, DIY crafts, hand lettering, and now rock painting!

Over the past couple of years, Kati has had the fantastic opportunity to lend her coloring and crafting talents to the adult coloring/zentangle/crafting publication *DO Magazine*, as well as to the artwork of many talented artists and designers including Valerie McKeehan of Lily & Val, Ben Kwok, Vera Bradley, Thaneeya McArdle, Jess Volinski, and Hello Angel.

She continues to reside in her home sweet hometown with two pesky (and absolutely adorable) fur-balls, Russell and Athena, who grasp at all chances to lay across, swat at, and/or spill liquid on any art project they can.

You can browse Kati's day-to-day artistic musings on her Instagram page, @quite.transfixed.

Also by Kati Erney!

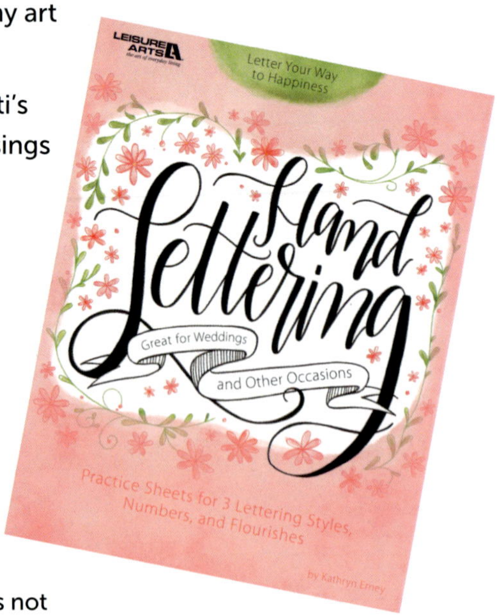

 Production Team: Technical Editor – Jean Lewis; Senior Graphic Artist – Lora Puls; Photo Stylist – Lori Wenger; Photographer – Jason Masters

Made in U.S.A.